T0289022

OLE HENDRICKS
AND HIS TUNEBOOK

Languages and Folklore of the Upper Midwest

JOSEPH SALMONS AND JAMES P. LEARY, *Series Editors*

Published in collaboration with the Center for the
Study of Upper Midwestern Cultures at the
University of Wisconsin–Madison

OLE HENDRICKS AND HIS TUNEBOOK

Folk Music and Community on the Frontier

Amy M. Shaw

THE UNIVERSITY OF WISCONSIN PRESS

Publication of this book has been made possible, in part,
through support from the Scandinavian Folk Arts and Cultural Traditions in the
Upper Midwest fellowship program of the American-Scandinavian Foundation.

The University of Wisconsin Press
728 State Street, Suite 443
Madison, Wisconsin 53706
uwpress.wisc.edu

Gray's Inn House, 127 Clerkenwell Road
London ECIR 5DB, United Kingdom
eurospanbookstore.com

Printed in the United States of America
This book may be available in a digital edition.

Library of Congress Cataloging-in-Publication Data
Names: Shaw, Amy M., author. | Hendricks, Ole, 1851–1935.
Title: Ole Hendricks and his tunebook : folk music and community on the
frontier / Amy M. Shaw.
Other titles: Languages and folklore of the Upper Midwest.
Description: Madison, Wisconsin : The University of Wisconsin Press, [2020] |
Series: Languages and folklore of the Upper Midwest |
Includes bibliographical references and index.
Identifiers: LCCN 2019052245 | ISBN 9780299328702 (cloth)
Subjects: LCSH: Hendricks, Ole, 1851–1935. | Fiddlers—Middle West—
Biography. | Norwegian Americans—Music—History and criticism. |
Folk music—Middle West—History and criticism. | Fiddle tunes. |
Folk music—Middle West.
Classification: LCC ML418.H46 S53 2020 | DDC 787.2/1620977—dc23
LC record available at https://lccn.loc.gov/2019052245

Handwritten music manuscripts by common Americans contain primary and direct evidence of their musical preferences during a particular time and in a particular place. To see, play from, or study one of these old manuscripts brings us as close to that person's musical life as history allows. Laborious inscriptions of a tune, hymn, or song—made by musicians of the music they played, loved, or wanted to learn—are precious and unique windows into music-making, acknowledging that this music mattered to them and, thus, matters to us!

—American Vernacular Music Manuscripts, ca. 1730–1910,
http://popmusic.mtsu.edu/ManuscriptMusic/

Mr. Hendricks, since coming here last summer, has done much towards building up this town, and is a most valuable acquisition to musical circles.

—*Grant County Herald*, November 20, 1890

Contents

Illustrations

Foreword

In this book, Amy Shaw gives us an exemplary case study, a virtuosic demonstration of how close examination of a single modest body of evidence can illuminate broad topics in music and cultural history. This is an extraordinary volume for three reasons. First, there is the useful timing of Ole Hendricks's activity. He fiddled toward the end of the nineteenth century, after the era when enough music commonplace books were penned to tell us about fiddlers' tastes. The heyday of this practice was from soon after the Revolutionary War through the 1840s. At that time, enlarged, newly cheap collections of fiddle tunes largely obviated the need to write down tunes by hand. The ever-expanding nature of published collections of fiddle tunes lowered their value as evidence of what fiddlers actually played; these assemblages of melodies became crudely cumulative rather than documents illustrating both creation and demise within fiddlers' repertoires. This created a sort of evidentiary desert that lasted until radio and recordings shot into prominence in the 1920s and after, revealing transformed and regionally differentiated practices. Hendricks's manuscript—a substantial music commonplace book compiled decades after the waning of making those—fits neatly into the late nineteenth-century gap in information concerning the history of American fiddling.

Second, Hendricks's collection offers pockets of very specific information concerning aspects of fiddling from his era. Instructive comparisons can be made with the hefty manuscript compilations of William Sidney Mount—best known as portraitist and genre painter but an avid semiprofessional fiddler, too—and even more pertinently, those of Charles M. Cobb, machinist, fiddler, and later wind-band leader active in rural Vermont from the

1840s through the 1890s. (Both men's collections are largely antebellum.) Mount, Cobb, and Hendricks (much later) gathered quadrilles/cotillions (synonyms) rather desperately, needing to serve their audiences' desires for long stretches of dancing to new music. The emphasis in all three men's collections was on quantity, though quadrilles such as #11 in this collection can grab our ears as firmly as do the dance tunes from later in Hendricks's manuscript. Of particular historical interest is how the quadrille had come to be more like the other pan-European genres of polkas, waltzes, and the like in terms of form as articulated by key, meter, and internal melodic relationships; it's a treat to compare Hendricks's quadrilles with the cotillions published decades earlier by Elias Howe. Hendricks played many technically challenging pieces, notably waltzes resembling those by Bohemian Josef Labitsky (1801–82), which were anthologized much earlier by Mount and Cobb. I am unsurprised by the left-hand agility required to perform Hendricks's repertoire; Mount, Cobb, and their many source fiddlers evinced this, too, in legions of tunes requiring third position (often plus extended fourth finger). Also, many of Hendricks's tunes are in hard keys, on both the flat and sharp sides. It may seem puzzling at first that Hendricks wrote down no mazurkas and very few tunes in D major, the commonest key throughout the history of American (and of Norwegian) fiddling. Part of his repertoire was likely housed exclusively in his memory. Another possible or partial explanation could resemble how we infer the existence of distant planets through observing anomalies in the orbits of other ones: Hendricks may have owned published collections that his music commonplace book complemented.

Third, this collection likely reflects general factors in the history of the Upper Midwest. It focuses on some of the region's old-time musical genres presented in a format that had become rare, in a part of the United States that tended to be old-fashioned due to its relatively late settlement. Much of the population consisted of immigrants who worked hard and were careful with their money, but who still wanted to hear music and to dance. Hendricks's repertoire also illustrates the conflation of the microregional cultures of Norway in this new home, and neatly balances the persistence of old-country with American musical materials. Readers will enjoy the chance to savor how the positive (and fascinating) Norwegian ingredients helped enrich life in the Upper Midwest in the decades flanking the turn of the twentieth century. More than a century later, we are living in an era when contributions to the economic, moral, and aesthetic textures of American life by contemporary immigrants need to be recognized and honored.

Chris Goertzen, University of Southern Mississippi

Preface

This book is an edition of a late nineteenth-century music manuscript compiled by the Norwegian-born fiddler Ole Hendricks (1851–1935). Containing some 124 dance tunes, his manuscript is an important primary source for the study of music and dance in immigrant communities in the rural Upper Midwest. This volume, intended for listeners, musicians, and researchers, provides transcriptions of these tunes and contextualizes them. It also tells the story of one immigrant's experience as shaped by various currents in American history.

This project could not have been completed without the generosity of Beth Rotto, who turned me loose on this rare tunebook in the first place and assisted me in so many ways; Chris Bashor, who read many, many drafts; Tammy Hendricks Creasy, who responded to my first inquiry on Ancestry.com and has been enthusiastic ever since; and James P. Leary, whose wise guidance was crucial. I would also like to thank Chris Goertzen, Paul Tyler, Laura Ellestad, and Amy Boxrud for their immensely helpful advice and encouragement. I am deeply grateful to all of you, as well as to everyone at the University of Wisconsin Press who helped make this volume a reality, especially Amber Cederström, Adam Mehring, Joseph Salmons, Mary Sutherland, Jennifer Conn, and Kaitlin Svabek. I was very fortunate to receive significant support for this project through a Folk Arts and Cultural Traditions fellowship from the American-Scandinavian Foundation; additional support was provided by the Sons of Norway Foundation.

Many others generously provided research assistance, pieces of information, or referrals at critical junctures. In Norway, Thomas Nilssen of Løten, Mary Barthelemy of Røros, Thor Ola Engen of Vallset, and Leif Ingvar

Rangøien, Music Archivist at Glomdalsmuseet in Elverum, were extremely helpful. In the United States, I was assisted by Patty Benson of the Grant County Historical Society, Paul Dahlin, Bob Douglas, Jim Hove, James Kimball of the State University of New York–Geneseo, Sabine Klaus of the National Music Museum, Michelle Koth of the Yale Music Library, Anna Rue and Jeanette Casey of the University of Wisconsin–Madison, Carl Rahkonen of the Indiana University of Pennsylvania Music Library, Valerie Thompson of Fergus Falls, the staff of the Gale Family Library of the Minnesota Historical Society, and my library colleagues Jade Erickson and Nathan Farley in St. Paul.

Mary Barthelemy also provided many translations, as did Jon-Anders Persson. Kari Grønningsæter, assisted by Astrid Roe, made a special trip to Sauherad to seek out Ole's former home near Klevar and take photographs. Charlie Langton of Vesterheim Museum photographed Ole's fiddle—a tricky process, indeed! Brian Donahue of bedesign, inc. provided graphic design assistance along the way. The inspiring epigraph from the American Vernacular Music Manuscripts project was written by Dale Cockrell, one of the project's co-directors; the Center for Popular Music at Middle Tennessee State University kindly allowed me to reproduce it here. For encouragement throughout this project, I would also like to thank Terry and Laurie Cochran, John Creasy, Beverly Foster, John Goodin, Sherry and Don Ladig, Laura MacKenzie, Marilyn McGriff, Bill Musser, Phil Nusbaum, Eric and Rosa Peltoniemi, Jon Rotto, Mary Shaw, Véronique St-Louis, Ross Sutter, and Martha Vest.

My musical collaborators in the New Ole Hendricks Orchestra have been instrumental (in both senses of the word) in reviving Ole's music for a new generation of listeners. Thank you, Vidar Skrede, Beth Rotto, Chris Bashor, David Tousley, and special guests, Bob Douglas and Ann Streufert, for working so hard on all those tunes!

OLE HENDRICKS
AND HIS TUNEBOOK

Introduction

On a chilly evening in late autumn, a lean man carrying a fiddle case strode down the wood sidewalk of a young town. Were it not so dark already, a bystander might have recognized that this was not a man with a desk job, as Ole's face bore the effects of years of working in the fields in all weathers. He stopped in front of a saloon, unlocked the front door, and went inside. The town had voted dry again, and the building stood empty, silent—but it would not remain so for long. He set the fiddle case down on the bar and proceeded to light a fire in the massive iron stove. Once the blaze was roaring, he went upstairs and made his way across the wooden dance floor, skirting a bull fiddle that lay on its side next to the small stage. Ole set his fiddle down beside his chair and went to light the kerosene lamps. The rest of the orchestra filed in—Ole's brother Halvor and fellow Norwegians Swen Olson and O. K. Thompson. Jack McQuillan, the lone Irishman of the group, soon joined them. People from the town and neighboring townships trickled in, everyone in high spirits. Before long the hall was a hubbub of conversation in Norwegian, Swedish, English. A few children ran across the floor, squealing. Ole extracted a music notebook from his case and placed it on the music stand. He had a new waltz he was eager to play. The week had been a hectic one—his three-year-old son had managed to fall down the cellar stairs, by some miracle avoiding serious injury[1]—but as Ole rosined his bow he felt the familiar surge of energy. While the musicians tuned their instruments, the floor manager shooed the kids off the floor, and the caller had the dancers form squares for quadrilles. When the squares were complete, the floor manager nodded to the musicians, Ole kicked off the first tune, and the dancers were off.

This is how I imagine many a Saturday night in Elbow Lake, Minnesota, a small town in the Red River Valley, during the waning years of the nineteenth century. Long before anyone was using the term "building community," Ole Hendricks was doing just that. Although he had a farm to run, various business interests to manage, and twelve children to raise, Ole somehow found time to play for many dances and social events in Elbow Lake and the surrounding area in Grant County. In the days before radio and recorded music were readily available, Ole's music was more than mere entertainment. It helped residents feel less isolated and encouraged them to connect with each other—in short, to feel at home in this fairly new community. No recordings of his playing have come to light; however, Ole did compile a manuscript book of dance tunes, which has survived to our day. This tunebook is an "immigrant trunkful" of music in a variety of styles, and it reveals much about music and dance in an area populated predominantly by people of Norwegian descent. Furthermore, the technical difficulty of many of the tunes he collected gives some insight into Ole's abilities as a fiddler. Had he not been capable of playing them, he probably would not have gone to the trouble of writing them down. His local newspaper once dubbed Ole "our violinist," and apparently he lived up to the title.[2]

That this rare tunebook survived at all is another miracle. Its provenance was first recounted to me by its current steward, Beth Hoven Rotto of Decorah, Iowa, in 2013. Beth is the fiddler in the band Foot-Notes, which for more than twenty-five years has done much to preserve traditional Norwegian American dance music from northeastern Iowa. The band's repertoire, harking back to the days of house parties and barn dances in the Upper Midwest, owes much to Beth's efforts to collect tunes from a variety of local musicians. Some of these tunes were featured on the Foot-Notes recording *My Father Was a Fiddler*.[3] This compact disc sparked the interest of people who had tunebooks, scrapbooks, and other musical heirlooms at home, and one of these collectors was a man living in Wisconsin named Orvin Svien.

Here is how the story began, as Beth tells it: "Some time after my band, Foot-Notes, made a recording of obscure tunes collected mostly from daughters of fiddlers from my area of northeast Iowa, I was contacted by a man named Orv Svien. He said he enjoyed that recording and was coming to Decorah to show me a violin. Not knowing anything about him, I asked him to meet me at my workplace. He arrived and showed me a unique-looking fiddle and told me enough of the story of Ole Hendricks that I asked him to sit down and tell me more."[4]

Because this story begins with a fiddle, the instrument itself warrants a closer look. It was unusual in that it has no overhang where the top and the back meet the ribs. The smooth, continuous curve here makes the instrument seem edgeless. While no label is present inside, the design is similar to that of a mid-nineteenth-century Russian luthier named Rigart (or Rigat) Rubus, who worked in St. Petersburg.[5] Sometimes referred to as "folk violins," the Rubus sound has been described as powerful but too unrefined for classical playing. Nonetheless, Ole clearly loved this instrument. Since he often played for a floor crowded with dancers before the days of amplification, perhaps what he sought was an instrument that could project. A violin specialist in Green Bay, Wisconsin, when consulted by Orv Svien, concluded this example was either an original Rubus or a copy.[6] Many of these copies, referred to as "Russian model," were made in Markneukirchen, Germany, during the second half of the nineteenth century. Ole's fiddle lacks the unconventional scroll typical of a Rubus and is probably one of these German copies.[7] The Minnesota luthier Paul Dahlin told me that he has encountered a few edgeless violins in the course of his long career, most of them of German manufacture. He remarked on the difficulty of repairing them: the lack of overhang makes it difficult to remove the top or the back.[8] Ole's instrument was destined to require major repairs.

Continuing with Beth Rotto's account, she states: "[Orv Svien] told me that Ole was an outstanding fiddler, whose fame extended from Minnesota into North Dakota, who played with [Orv's] uncle Andrew."[9] Andrew Svien (1881–1965) was a longtime resident of Grant County. His family, originally from Vang in Oppland in central Norway, came to Grant County from Goodhue County, Minnesota, in 1896.[10] The Sviens and Hendrickses were not close neighbors, but both families farmed land in Pomme de Terre township.[11] Ole and Andrew became good friends. According to Orv, Andrew was a champion fiddler, well-known across the region, "but as good as he was, he had to play second [fiddle] for Ole."[12]

Ole Hendricks died on October 14, 1935. According to Beth, Orv told her that "Ole had developed cancer and when the pain was unbearable he sat along a river bank, played his fiddle for a while, then shot himself to

Figure 1. Ole Hendricks's Russian model violin, in the style of Rigart Rubus of St. Petersburg, Russia. The instrument has corners and purfling but no distinct edges where the top and back meet the ribs. Photographs by Charlie Langton.

death. He fell onto his revolver, cracking the back of his fiddle."[13] Piecing together the facts of Ole's death is difficult at this late date. However, he was living in Isanti County in eastern Minnesota at that time, and it was probably on the shore of Lake Fannie where he died. Ole's grandson Quentin Hendricks related a story that came from his uncle, Ole's son Henry: "[Lake Fannie] was Grandpa Ole's favorite fishing hole, but he never fished when he [went there]. He told Grandma Elizabeth that he was going fishing, giving him a more legitimate reason to leave the farm work [to] go and try to catch something for supper. So he would take his fishing pole and his fiddle and head to Lake Fannie. Uncle Henry went on to say that Grandpa Ole died doing what he enjoyed most: fiddlin' at the fishin' hole."[14] Ole was buried in the cemetery at Spring Lake Lutheran in Isanti County. His remains were later reinterred at Hillside Cemetery in Minneapolis next to his wife, Elizabeth, when she died in 1947.

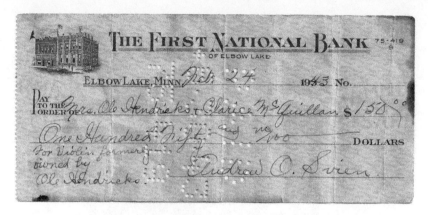

Figure 2. Andrew Svien's payment for Ole Hendricks's fiddle, dated February 24, 1943. Courtesy of Beth Hoven Rotto.

In 1943, some seven years after Ole died, Andrew Svien purchased Ole's fiddle for $150 from the family. The fiddle was still in its damaged state; Ole's daughter Clarice McQuillan remarked in a letter to Andrew, "It will cost you quite a bit by the time you get it repaired."[15]

Despite its problematic design, the fiddle was duly repaired at William Lewis & Son in Chicago and continued on its journey.[16] As told by Beth Rotto:

When Andrew died, the fiddle was passed down to his son [Orwell Svien, a music teacher], and when that son died [in 1980], the fiddle was auctioned as part of the estate. Orv asked relatives who were planning to attend the sale to try to purchase the fiddle for him. After the sale, when he asked about it, they said there had been a fiddle there, but it had a patch in the back and didn't look like much. They did, however, know who had purchased it, a Mrs. Brown. Mrs. Brown was contacted and she said that she would sell the violin to Orv for the price she paid for it—$20. The tunebook came with the fiddle.

Orv told me that Ole's fiddle needed playing, and that he wanted to loan it to me. I was reluctant, but he insisted. A few days later he contacted me to say that he actually wanted to give me the violin. Orv sent me a copy of the Ole Hendricks tunebook and made copies for several other fiddlers and Garrison Keillor. That was back in 2001. It was just a few years ago, before

Orv passed away in 2015 at age 97, that he sent me the original tunebook. When Orv understood that we were preparing to tell Ole's story and bring his music back to light, he also located a photo of Ole and Uncle Andrew with their fiddles.[17]

And that is how this hundred-year-old tunebook, after passing through numerous hands, was entrusted to Beth Rotto, and how this project all

Figure 3. Ole Hendricks (*right*) with Andrew Svien. Courtesy of Beth Hoven Rotto.

began. I did not know all these details when I first heard about Ole Hendricks; some came out in my subsequent research. However, Beth's story of this immigrant fiddler was irresistible to me as a researcher and musician. I wanted to know more about Ole, the times he lived in, and this fascinating tunebook that had somehow escaped oblivion. Beth generously shared the manuscript with me and encouraged me at every step of this project. I located some of Ole's descendants early on. Their impression of him, based on the information passed down through the family, was that he had not been much of a success as a farmer. They were unaware that Ole had been a fiddler, a good one. Not surprisingly, there are still musicians in the family, and they were thrilled to hear there was another side to him. I eagerly set out to uncover the rest of the story. Piecing it together proved to be challenging due to the small number of extant primary sources coming directly from Ole himself. As far as I am aware, he left no recordings, not many photographs, and very few written materials other than the tunebook itself. Musical notation has its limitations—it does not communicate exactly how Ole interpreted or used these tunes in actual practice. Still, there was much to be learned through a careful examination of the available evidence.

What follows is essentially a case study of a single immigrant fiddler and the music he collected. Chapter 1 traces Ole's life from his beginnings in Norway to the height of his musical activity as a dance musician in Elbow Lake, Minnesota. Chapter 2 delves into the music he played for local dancers as evidenced by what is contained in his remarkable tunebook. Chapter 3 continues the story of Ole's life from his later years in Elbow Lake to his retirement years in his subsequent home of North Branch, Minnesota. These chapters set the stage for the transcriptions of the actual tunes, with their annotations, in Part 2.

As a mindfulness exercise, students of Buddhist philosophy are sometimes asked to consider a single leaf and to see that the leaf is not just a plant—it is also the sunshine, the air, the clouds, the rain, the soil, and all the other things that interact to bring the leaf into being. Similarly, Ole's tunebook is not merely a paper notebook with some music written in it. With some imagination, you can perceive an immigrant family on an epic journey, multicultural communities in the Upper Midwest, and a panoply of musicians, composers, and dancers in the Old World and the New.

PART I

The Life and Music of Ole Hendricks

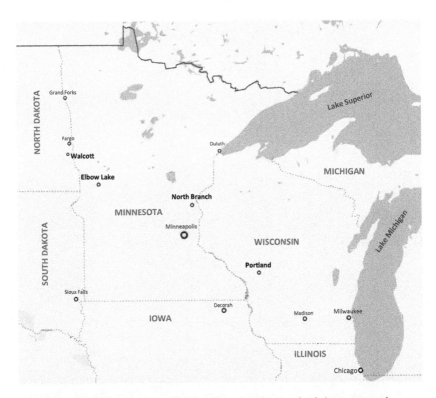

Figure 4. Map of the Upper Midwest showing Ole Hendricks's successive homes: Portland in Monroe County, Wisconsin; Walcott, in Richland County in present-day North Dakota; Elbow Lake, in Grant County, Minnesota; and North Branch Township, in Isanti County, Minnesota.

CHAPTER ONE

From Norway to a
Little Dance Hall on the Prairie

Ole (Olav) Andrew Hendricks was born on February 19, 1851, on a croft (tenant farm) named Neset under Gvannes, in Sauherad Parish, Telemark. He was the fifth of nine children born to Andreas Hendriksen (1814–85), who was a *husmann* (a cotter, or tenant farmer), and Helga (Helge) Olsdatter (1815–91).[1]

Figure 5. Ole Hendricks's father was a husmann at the farm named Klevar near Sauherad. This photo shows nearby Hågenn, where his family's cottage would have stood in the woods. Courtesy of Kari Grønningsæter.

Figure 6. Stabbur (storehouse) at Klevar dating from the thirteenth century. One of the oldest in the country, it stands as it did when the family left Hågenn. These buildings, which were mounted on posts to keep out dampness and vermin, were used by landowners to store grain, flour, smoked meats, etc. Courtesy of Kari Grønningsæter.

Times were hard in Norway, especially for *husmenn*, most of whom had little hope of ever owning their own farms. Arable land was scarce and job opportunities limited, and the growing population exacerbated this situation. As described by Odd Lovoll, "Conditions were crowded on the small farms in the Norwegian fjord and mountain districts. These tradition-bound farming communities were not able to increase production to keep pace with the rapid growth in population, and pursuing a better life in America became the solution for many."[2] Between 1825 and 1925 approximately 850,000 Norwegians immigrated, most of them settling in rural areas across the Upper Midwest.[3]

Andreas, Helga, and their six children left Norway in May or early June 1854, during the first great wave of immigration.[4] Ole was then three years old. They would have boarded a sailing ship, perhaps in Oslo or in nearby

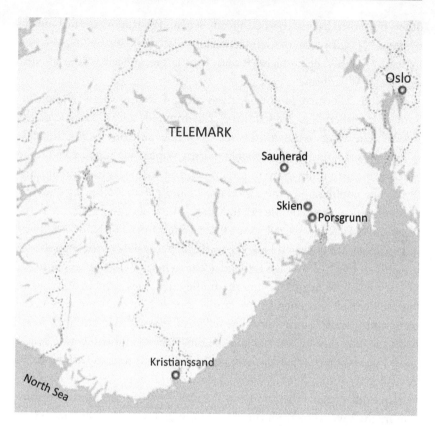

Figure 7. Map of Norway, showing Ole Hendricks's birthplace at Sauherad, Telemark, and some possible ports of departure.

Skien or Porsgrunn. Probably traveling in steerage, they would have endured an uncomfortable passage across the Atlantic that often took six to eight weeks. Most immigrants from Norway at this time entered the United States through ports in Quebec. One common route west from Quebec City was to take a river steamer to Hamilton on Lake Ontario, and from there travel by rail to Chicago by way of Detroit.[5]

From Chicago, the Hendriksen family might first have gone to one of the big Norwegian settlements, such as Koshkonong in southern Wisconsin, to get their bearings before continuing to their final destination. Eventually the family settled in what later became Portland Township in Monroe County, Wisconsin. Usually Norwegians were attracted to places where others from their home areas had already settled. Portland was settled mostly by people of Norwegian or German ancestry. Telemark was well represented in nearby Coon Valley, which has one of the largest concentrations of Norwegians in Wisconsin.[6]

Portland is located in the Driftless area of southwestern Wisconsin. Sometimes called "Coulee Country," this forested, hilly landscape might have felt like home to the new arrivals from Telemark, but during the mid- to late 1850s it would have been only sparsely populated. Supplies had to be purchased thirty miles away in La Crosse, and there was no church until 1874.[7] The population in the region grew rapidly in the following decades, no doubt encouraged by the rail line from Milwaukee to La Crosse, completed in 1858, which passed about fifteen miles from Portland.[8] Ole lived in Portland until he was at least thirty. By 1877, the date of the map shown in figure 9, Ole had his own farm adjacent to his father Andreas's farm.

Ole must have begun playing the fiddle during his years in Wisconsin, but whether he was taught by a family member or someone else in the community remains a mystery. The technical mastery evident in the tune-book suggests that he was not self-taught; someone probably gave him a good foundation. Certainly, there could have been musical neighbors in Portland: according to oral history collected by Philip Martin, many Norwegian fiddlers made their home in the Driftless area.[9] Additional inspiration might have come from the great Norwegian violinist Ole Bull (1810–80). Between 1870 and 1880, Bull spent some time in Madison, Wisconsin, having married the daughter of a Wisconsin senator. The young Ole Hendricks might or might not have had the opportunity to hear him, but Bull's performing activities were reported in Wisconsin newspapers and were no doubt a source of pride to the Norwegian immigrant community.[10]

The existence of two fiddling traditions in Norway may provide a clue to Ole's early training. At the time the family emigrated, strong regional traditions of *hardingfele* (Hardanger fiddle) playing existed in parts of Norway. In fact, their home parish of Sauherad produced some of the finest players of the Hardanger. For example, Torgeir Augundsson (1801–72), nicknamed Myllarguten, and Lars Fykerud (1860–1902), both legendary artists of the Hardanger fiddle, were born in Sauherad.[11] This instrument is similar to the regular fiddle, but its lowest bowed string is often tuned a step lower, and a great variety of other Hardanger tunings are known. In

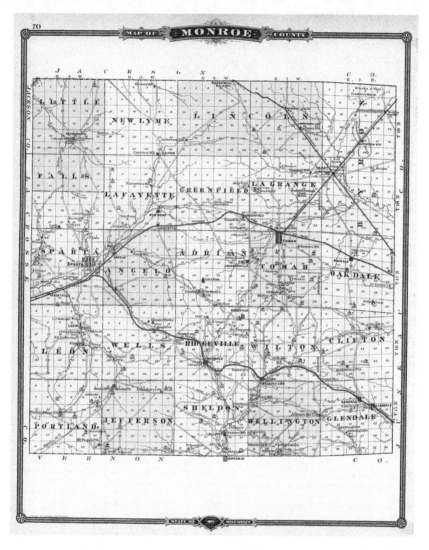

Figure 8. Monroe County, Wisconsin, in 1878 with Portland Township in the southwest corner. Courtesy of the David Rumsey Map Collection, David Rumsey Map Center, Stanford Libraries.

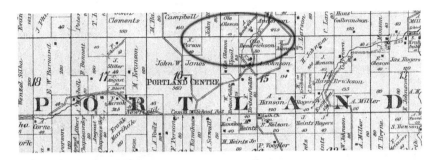

Figure 9. Map of Portland, Monroe County, Wisconsin, in 1877 showing location of farms owned by Andreas Hendrickson and his son Ole. Courtesy of the New York Public Library.

addition to its bowed strings, the Hardanger fiddle has four or five unbowed strings running under the fingerboard that vibrate in sympathy, lending increased resonance to the sound. Traditionally decorated with inked designs or with inlaid bone or shell, the instrument became a national symbol of Norway. Despite the fact that Sauherad was "Hardanger fiddle country," there is no evidence that Ole ever played anything but the regular fiddle. Since he came from an area where the regular fiddle was uncommon, this suggests that he learned to fiddle not from family members or even from musicians from Telemark but from musicians coming from other parts of Norway where the regular fiddle was more common.[12] When one examines the contents of the tunebook more closely, its numerous connections to the Hedmark region in eastern Norway become apparent.

Of course, Ole's musical literacy could have been fostered in a variety of other ways. In America, he would encounter musicians from other ethnic backgrounds. Howard Marshall, in his study of fiddling in Missouri, notes that German immigrant music "professors" played an important role in the music education of many fiddlers. Considering the sizable contingent of German immigrants in Portland, it is easy to imagine that one of them may been a music master who provided lessons. Marshall also credits the American band movement in the development of many fiddlers, and, as Victor Greene points out, Germans and Bohemians brought strong brass band traditions with them to Wisconsin.[13] Ole almost certainly gained musical knowledge while playing in a brass band during his youth, since he went on to play in the town band in Elbow Lake. Like many in nineteenth-century America, he might also have participated in singing schools, where the rudiments of music were taught from songbooks or hymnals.[14] In addition, many tune anthologies from publishers such as Elias Howe in Boston included material designed to teach note-reading, violin bowing, etc., to the autodidact.

WESTWARD TO DAKOTA TERRITORY

In 1880, Ole married Elizabeth Peterson, who was born in Wisconsin to Norwegian parents.[15] By 1884, the couple and their two young children had relocated to Dakota Territory. They settled in the new community of Walcott in Richland County in the southeast corner of present-day North Dakota.[16]

Several factors probably influenced Ole's move to Dakota. By the later 1870s, the succession of Indian wars had ended, as had the swarms of locusts that had wreaked havoc on crops across the plains.[17] Railroads expanded dramatically over the next decade, providing convenient transportation into the territory and making it possible to transport crops to distant markets. The railroads also owned vast tracts of land in Dakota, which soon became settlements and towns. Walcott itself was established on land that had been owned by the Northern Pacific Railroad. Ole might have been swayed by the aggressive marketing strategies of the railroads, newspapers, and territorial Board of Immigration. The board, for example, sent representatives to Wisconsin to distribute Norwegian-language promotional materials and to exhibit impressive samples of Dakota produce, such as seven-pound turnips, at agricultural fairs. An unusual amount of rain fell across the Great Plains between 1878 and 1886, leading to the myth that rain follows the plow.[18] In 1879, the *Fargo Times* distributed 40,000 copies of a special edition highlighting the merits of the Red River Valley.[19]

Ole's younger brother, Halvor, moved to Walcott first and no doubt encouraged Ole to follow him.[20] Soon Ole joined the mass exodus of 1878–87, which became known as the Great Dakota Boom. With land prices rising farther east, cheap land was a huge draw.[21] By 1889, people of Norwegian background made up 87 percent of the population of Walcott.[22]

Ole might not have gone to Walcott with the sole intent of farming. In his spare time, he was certainly playing music. In fact, it was the Walcott correspondent for the *Richland County Gazette* who referred to him as "our

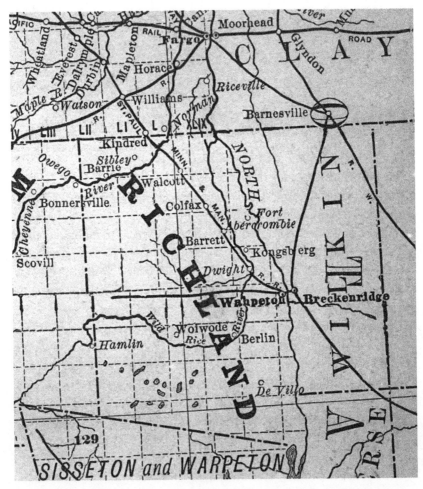

Figure 10. Detail from a map of Dakota Territory, showing the location of Walcott, about twenty-five miles south of Fargo. Library of Congress, Geography and Map Division.

violinist." It seems likely that Ole played for dances as a member of the Steelhammer Orchestra.[23] This ensemble was led by a Swedish-born blacksmith aptly named Andrew G. Steelhammer.[24] Andrew was said to be "one of the most prominent and respected men of the place" as well as a shrewd mechanic, and people enjoyed gathering around the fire at his smithy.[25] Ole and the older Andrew were neighbors and probably friends, and it is reasonable to assume that they also played music together.[26]

While many Dakotans of Norwegian descent were pro-temperance, Ole was not of this persuasion. Shortly after his move to Walcott, Ole opened what was probably his first saloon, in partnership with Halvor. Perhaps the fiddle was an asset to Ole as a saloon owner. Philip Martin has remarked that those proprietors who "kept a fiddle hanging in the bar and knew how to use it" could create a welcoming atmosphere.[27] The bar was certainly in operation by May 1884, when it was mentioned in the minutes of the county commissioners.[28] In the 1885 territorial census, both Ole and Halvor are recorded as being saloonkeepers, not farmers. Their liquor license was renewed by the county commissioners in January 1886; however, that license was short lived, since the county promptly voted dry during the fall election. The *Richland County Gazette* columnist had some fun at Ole's expense: "Walcott is a temperance village. Nothing stronger than lemonade and ginger ale can be found at Ole Hendrick's [*sic*] temperance saloon."[29] In 1887, Richland County once again legalized liquor.[30] So began a recurrent theme: Ole would attempt to operate a saloon, while the county voted

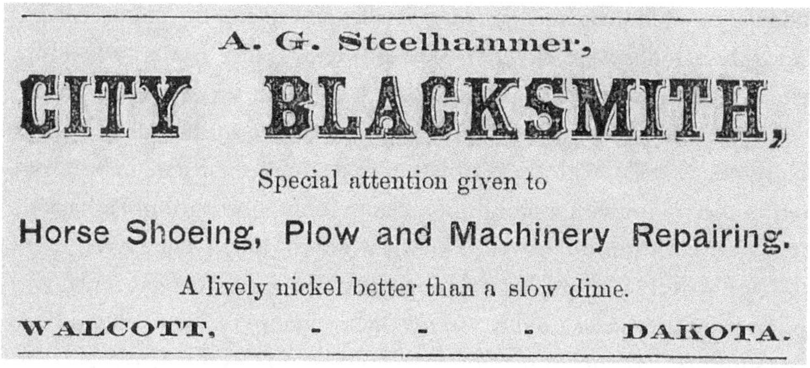

Figure 11. Advertisement placed by Andrew Steelhammer in Horace B. Crandall's *A History of Richland County* (1886). Courtesy of the HathiTrust.

alternately wet or dry. The pro-temperance faction was always close at his heels. He was granted another license in January 1889, to the chagrin of several anti-liquor activists who had submitted a remonstrance.[31] The Walcott correspondent quipped, "Messrs. [John] Nord and Hendricks are not building an ice palace, but are getting ready to ice palates next summer."[32]

RELOCATION TO ELBOW LAKE

In 1890, Ole again followed Halvor, this time eastward across the border to Elbow Lake in Grant County, Minnesota. Elbow Lake was about sixty miles from Walcott, and by 1887, the year his brother moved there, a good network of rail lines existed in the area, enabling convenient travel between the two communities.[33] Musical groups from Elbow Lake performed in Walcott and vice versa.[34] Grant County was also heavily populated by people of Norwegian background.[35]

What prompted Ole to pull up stakes? Significant crop failures in Walcott in 1887 were followed by a severe drought in 1889.[36] Prohibition was another factor. As early as March 1887 (one of the dry years in Richland County), the *Gazette* columnist remarked, "An epidemic has been prevailing in Walcott this spring, called the Elbow Lake fever. Upon the first appearance of the fever, it was not considered contagious, but it soon spread, until nearly every one had a slight attack. Some few cases proved fatal, but those who thought they could do without a saloon license have nearly recovered."[37] Nevertheless, by the summer of 1887, the *Wahpeton Times* reported that the population of Walcott was "growing smaller and smaller . . . [e]specially . . . since the saloons were closed."[38] The pro-temperance faction was all too effective in hindering the livelihood of our erstwhile saloonkeeper. The last straw must have been when North Dakota became a full-fledged state on November 2, 1889, with the distinction of being the first state to be admitted to the Union with a prohibition clause in its constitution. Perhaps the new state constitution provoked another bout of Elbow Lake fever!

Ole's arrival in Elbow Lake during the summer of 1890 was noted with interest by the *Grant County Herald*: "Mr. Hendricks, since coming here last summer, has done much towards building up this town, and is a most valuable acquisition to musical circles."[39] By the fall, Ole had a house ready for his family, and they all joined him in Elbow Lake.[40]

Ole wasted no time opening a saloon in partnership with Swen (Sven) Olson (1863–1943). Ole and Swen got along like the proverbial house on fire. Swen's trajectory was similar to Ole's: born in Norway, he came to this country as a small child, settling somewhere in Wisconsin, later moving to North Dakota, and finally winding up in Elbow Lake. In fact, they might have become acquainted some years earlier, since a twenty-two-year-old "Sven Olson" (or perhaps "Swan" Olson) is listed as part of Halvor Hendricks's household in Walcott in the 1885 Dakota territorial census. Swen moved to Elbow Lake in 1887, the same year as Halvor Hendricks. Swen had a head for business, and his acumen was probably vital to the partnership. Besides the saloon, Swen's numerous commercial interests in Grant County over the years included a bakery, a restaurant, a soda pop factory, and a wholesale liquor business. He had one of the earliest steam-powered threshing rigs in town.[41] For a time, he and Ole were partners in a farm machinery dealership (see fig. 14).[42]

Swen Olson was also a musician. He played string bass, cornet, and fiddle, and was Ole's frequent musical collaborator during these years. Besides playing for dances, Ole and Swen performed in the Elbow Lake Band, with Ole on baritone and Swen on cornet. Furthermore, Swen was likely the composer of three tunes in Ole's tunebook (#1a, #1b, and #9b).

Unfortunately, as in Walcott, the saloon in Elbow Lake was not in continuous operation. Here, too, the temperance issue was fiercely contested.[43] But the real significance of Ole and Swen's saloon is that it had a dance hall upstairs. In late November 1890, the local newspaper reported that "Olson & Hendricks are extending their building on Central avenue 24 feet, which will make the new building 24×64. The whole building will be made two stories high, the second story to be used for a dancing hall."[44]

The dance hall had a high ceiling, which enabled the installation of a stage curtain for theatricals, and the hall itself could accommodate about 150 people comfortably. Besides dances, the hall was used for plays, charity events, minstrel shows, town meetings, school events, lectures, and concerts by touring performers. The dances held there were significant social events. Often held on Friday or Saturday evenings or scheduled over a holiday, the dances were announced in the newspaper and tickets were sold in advance.

Figure 12. Swen Olson as pictured in *Illustrated Souvenir of Grant County* (1896). Courtesy of the Grant County Historical Society, Elbow Lake, Minnesota.

Figure 13. Saloon owned by Swen Olson (*far left*), possibly the one he operated with Ole Hendricks. Courtesy of the Grant County Historical Society, Elbow Lake, Minnesota.

Figure 14. Advertisement for Olson & Hendricks that appeared in the *Grant County Herald* for August 27, 1891. From the collections of the Minnesota Historical Society.

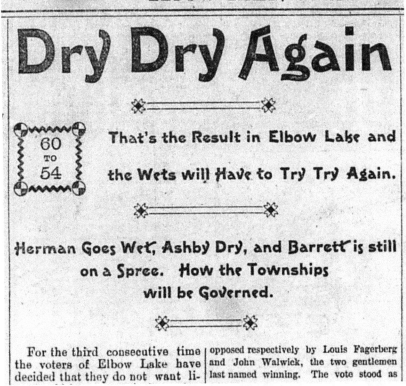

ELBOW LAKE, GRANT COU

Dry Dry Again

60 TO 54

That's the Result in Elbow Lake and the Wets will Have to Try Try Again.

Herman Goes Wet, Ashby Dry, and Barrett is still on a Spree. How the Townships will be Governed.

For the third consecutive time the voters of Elbow Lake have decided that they do not want li- | opposed respectively by Louis Fagerberg and John Walwick, the two gentlemen last named winning. The vote stood as

Figure 15. Headline in the *Grant County Herald* during one of the prohibition years (March 10, 1898). From the collections of the Minnesota Historical Society.

The music was provided by an orchestra variously called the Hendricks Orchestra, the Hendricks String Band, or Olson & Hendricks Orchestra. It was usually a four- or five-piece ensemble. Besides Ole and Swen, members over the years included Ole's brother, Halvor; Ole's two oldest children, Albert and Clara; O. K. (Ole) Thompson; John G. (Jack) McQuillan; and perhaps Andrew Svien.[45] Of this list, only McQuillan was not of Norwegian background. The instrumentation probably varied according to the membership, but at one time or another included violin, clarinet, cornet, string bass, and piano.

Figure 16. Dances sometimes followed other events at Olson & Hendricks Hall, such as this performance of the Norwegian play *Til sæters*, announced in the *Grant County Herald* on March 17, 1892. From the collections of the Minnesota Historical Society.

The first dance in the new hall was held on December 26, 1890, and was said to be "a complete success in all its arrangements. The hall itself is a fine addition to the general appearance of Elbow Lake and a source of convenience on public occasions."[46] Subsequent dances were soon announced with such remarks as "It would be superfluous to add that the music will be first class, for it always is when the Hendricks brothers have anything to do with it."[47]

A typical evening of dancing began at eight or nine o'clock in the evening and continued until about eleven or midnight when supper, often featuring oysters, was served in a nearby hotel or restaurant. Dancing would resume afterward and could go as late as two o'clock in the morning. Besides the orchestra, there was generally a dance caller and a floor manager. The floor manager's role was to make sure the sets were complete, find places for everybody who wanted to dance, tell the musicians when to start playing, and so forth.[48]

Groups such as fraternal organizations sometimes sponsored big, elaborate balls. These events were often described in detail in the next week's newspaper, as in the case of a ball held as part of a businessmen's banquet in 1893: "the dance hall was never before taxed to such an extent as on this evening, and while on ordinary occasions it is looked upon as a spacious and comfortable dance resort, it was entirely inadequate to accommodate the merry throng of dancers. Hendricks' full orchestra furnished the music, which was par excellence. The local band played several pieces to enliven the spirits of the crowd, after which the grand march was formed and the dance was soon in full blast."[49]

A more formal ball began with a grand march. It is unclear what specific music Ole selected for it, but in many places the grand march was a processional in $\frac{3}{4}$ time, a form with roots in the polonaise. Polonaises were certainly played in Norway, but Ole's tunebook contains no polonaises. According to Phil Jamison, the grand march typically began with all the couples promenading around the perimeter of the floor and then processing up the center of the hall toward the orchestra. When they reached the top, couples would peel off alternately to the left or right, go to the back of the line, process again as rows of two couples, peel off, return to the back of the line, process as rows of four couples, and so on until rows of eight couples were processing.[50]

Masquerade balls, at which there were prizes for the best costumes, were also popular at Olson & Hendricks's hall: "The private masquerade given by Mr. and Mrs. C. H. Downs on Monday evening was suberb [*sic*] in all its conceptions and appointments. About thirty suits were rented in the cities and home talent conceived some happy hits. . . . The dancing program was executed at Hendricks' hall to the music of the city's finest orchestra."[51] Some of the more striking disguises that night included Buffalo Bill, George Washington, a snow queen, a Norwegian flower girl, and a demon. Three people were dressed in Telemark costumes. There were even a few cross-dressers at some of these masquerades.

Besides playing in Olson & Hendricks's hall, Ole's orchestra sometimes played at dances in nearby towns. They were part-time musicians and seldom went farther than the neighboring townships, although they did travel on at least one occasion to Paynesville, Minnesota, about seventy-seven miles away.[52] As in other places around the Midwest, house parties closer to home were doubtless the scene of much music making, dancing, and socializing.[53] The neighborhood news columns in the *Grant County Herald* frequently mention dancing at house parties but rarely are any details given about the music. However, the following news item appeared in January 1900: "Ole Hendricks was the beneficiary of a surprise party Saturday evening. He was not expecting company and his first intimation that he was to act as host was the jingle of bells in his front yard. The party came to have a good time and they had it. The members of the Hendricks-Sand orchestra [a group formed by Ole's son Albert and Lars Sand] were nearly all present, and the music of the evening was fine."[54]

CHAPTER TWO

A Trove of Tunes

The music Ole played for these events is reflected in the contents of his tunebook. Beginning with its physical aspects, we find the tunebook was well-used: the corners of its pages have darkened as a result of handling, and the edges are ragged. Oblong in shape, it measures 17 cm (6.7 in) in height by 27 cm (10.6 in) in width. No title page or opening inscription inside the cover is present. The volume is hardcover, bound in plain cardboard binding, with forty-nine leaves of preprinted music manuscript paper, followed by one blank unlined leaf. Only one of the lined pages is blank—the ninety-eighth page at the very end of the book (although the pages are not consistently numbered). Most of the tunes bear a title or some other inscription in Norwegian or English. Tunes were added over time instead of being deliberately organized into sections, such as by tune type. All the music is instrumental; none includes lyrics.

One term used to describe documents like this is *vernacular music manuscript*. Another term used by musicologists, folklorists, and historians is *music commonplace book*. Commonplace books, as described by Chris Goertzen, "are individuals' compilations of memorabilia (proverbs, poems, recipes, or on occasion pieces of music) recorded by hand in previously bound blank books."[1] Ole's transcriptions include many complex tunes written in an "unhesitant" hand, featuring expressive indications such as dynamic markings, all of which suggests that he was often working from published or manuscript collections of music that were perhaps shared by friends or neighbors. In some cases, Ole's version of a tune is very similar to a known published version.

It is likely that other tunes in the collection were learned aurally from fellow musicians. Some tunes are notated in a simple, straightforward manner with no expressive markings. Another clue is that some tunes are notated imperfectly. Whereas folk musicians today are able to make a digital recording of a tune for future reference, Ole had no such helpful technology. After returning home from a musical gathering where he had heard something new, Ole had only his memory to rely on. For example, tune #38, Reinlender, seems to have been transcribed from a partial memory of a live performance or was a first draft that he never got around to correcting (see the annotation in Part 2 for details). Tunes #18c (a reel-like quadrille tune) and #26 (another reinlender) also have the appearance of early drafts. Another clue that some tunes may have been collected from live musicians is the degree to which they differ from other more common versions. For example, other versions of tune #30, Darkes Dream [Darkie's Dream], feature syncopations that are not present in Ole's version. Although this study necessarily focuses on the evidence in the tunebook, that he was musically literate would not have prevented Ole from playing older material in a traditional style that he had learned by ear. Ole's repertoire no doubt included additional tunes from the oral tradition that are not represented in his tunebook.

The tunebook was probably compiled between about 1880 and 1900, but I was not able to establish exact dates. While the bulk of it seems to date from Ole's years in Elbow Lake, he could have started it prior to moving there. Only two tunes are marked with a year: #51, Waltz No. 84 (1897) and #60, a waltz bearing the inscription "Elbow Lake 1891." These tunes appear in the second half of the book, suggesting that Ole had by then been collecting for quite some time. Therefore, he might have begun his compilation earlier, perhaps during the 1880s while he was in Walcott. An inscription on tune #66, Polka, indicates he was still living in Elbow Lake at the time he notated it. Five tunes toward the end of the book (#79a–d, 6th Lancers–Annette, and #80, Life Is a Dream Waltz) are based on sheet music that was published in the 1870s and 1880s, and thus are of little help in establishing a more exact completion date for the collection. The presence of a few tunes added in different hands (see Part 2 for examples) further complicates the dating. Because Ole's friend Andrew Svien did not write notation, according to his nephew Orvin Svien, it seems

Figure 17. Polka composed by Ole Hendricks, his only extant composition, on page [58] of the manuscript. Courtesy of Beth Hoven Rotto.

most likely that Ole's children, several of whom were musicians, added these tunes.[2]

At least one of the tunes seems to have been composed in Elbow Lake: #58, a polka composed by Ole himself. In addition, the three tunes composed by Swen Olson (#1a, #1b, and #9b) might also have been composed in Elbow Lake, but it is equally possible they were composed in Dakota Territory, if in fact Swen lived for a time in Walcott.

FIDDLE TUNES OR VIOLIN MUSIC?

Taken as a whole, Ole's tunebook can be viewed as reflecting several historical themes. One of these themes is the blurring of the distinction between the old-time fiddler and the classical violinist, which took place during the nineteenth century. Speaking of the early decades of the century, Goertzen describes it as "an age when vernacular fiddling overlapped considerably with pop and art music."[3] Versatility was the order of the day, according to Marshall, especially as settlers moved westward into sparsely populated areas: "Dance fiddlers often knew both classical and fiddling techniques and benefited from lessons with itinerant music teachers. . . . Fiddlers often embraced all forms of music and soaked up all the knowledge they could,

Figure 18. The first page of the tunebook, showing two tunes by Swen Olson. Courtesy of Beth Hoven Rotto.

which often meant learning to read music as well as absorbing through oral tradition in live performance."[4]

Many of the dance tunes Ole collected are indeed challenging to play. When I began this project, it was immediately apparent that these tunes were quite different from those one usually hears at Scandinavian festivals and dances in the Upper Midwest today. Three- and four-part tunes appear frequently in the collection, often with key changes in each part. In addition, the melodic range is distinctly wider. Many of the tunes require shifting into higher positions on the fingerboard, which is difficult for many traditional fiddlers today. Some of the tunes even extend to the high A above the staff. According to Bruce Bollerud of the Goose Island Ramblers, these wide-range tunes were more common in the days before brass instruments became prominent in dance bands.[5] Other technical challenges in Ole's tunes include rapid sixteenth-note passages, double stops, and triple stops. Furthermore, many of his tunes are violin-centric in that they are often set in so-called closed keys such as E or B-flat. These keys involve playing the open, unstopped strings less frequently, and are less conducive to playing double stops with one note on an open string—a technique for harmonizing a melody that is common in old-time fiddling. In short, many of these tunes are more "violinistic" in nature and would be difficult for any fiddler without the benefit of some formal training.

NORWEGIAN ROOTS

Ole's Norwegian roots are evident in his tunebook, but to understand this aspect of the manuscript it is important to note what is *not* present. Ole's tunebook reflects another historical theme: the decline of older regional styles of Norwegian traditional music following immigration. Back in Norway, the old *bygdedans* (village or regional dance) repertoire, usually played solo on the Hardanger fiddle or on the regular fiddle, was extremely local in character. This genre includes tunes that accompanied dances such as the *springar, gangar, halling, pols,* and *rull.* The manner of performing these dances and their music could vary from one valley to the next. For example, the springar, a triple-meter dance, has an asymmetric beat: the emphasized beat depended on the region.[6]

In the New World, these intricate bygdedans tunes and their associated dances, as unique and beautiful as they might appear to us now, began to fall by the wayside.[7] For one thing, the population was more diverse than in the old country. While Norwegians often settled in enclaves that persisted past the second generation, they did not live in complete isolation, and communities became more diverse as time went on. Elbow Lake was populated mostly by Norwegians who came from different areas of Norway—Trondheim, Stavanger, various districts in Buskerud, and southern Hedmark.[8] Census data shows they had neighbors who were Swedes, Danes, Germans, Anglo-Canadians, Irish, Scots, or Yankees who had relocated from farther east. As summed up by Odd Lovoll, "No township consisted of a single ethnic group."[9] If you were hosting a dance and wanted to be welcoming to the German neighbors who had just helped you raise your barn, the best way to get everyone out on the dance floor was not to strike up a springar or a halling.[10] Interestingly, not a single bygdedans tune can be found in Ole Hendricks's tunebook.

Gammaldans tunes

If bygdedans was increasingly rare, what brought the people of Elbow Lake out on the dance floor? Here, they were dancing to music represented in

Ole's tunebook—a genre that came to be called *gammaldans*. Loosely translated, the word means "old-time dance." This repertoire, however, is actually more recent than bygdedans and closer to the popular end of the musical spectrum. Gammaldans refers to a number of social dances and their music that became common across Europe and spread to Norway over the course of the nineteenth century—primarily the *vals, masurka, reinlender,* and polka.[11] While the solo musician held sway in bygdedans, gammaldans music is ensemble-based. The preferred term for this genre in much recent scholarship from Norway is *runddans* (round dance). This term refers to the circular turning technique common to all of these dance types, in which the partners stand face to face, hold on to each other, and turn together. Commercial activity (e.g., Norway's extensive timber exports to other countries), traveling musicians of Romany background, and musicians congregating at large country markets such as Grundset Fair, all contributed to the spread of this music.[12] According to Daniel Beal, some of these dances "were 'Norwegianized' almost beyond recognition."[13] The tunes themselves underwent a similar process: while not indigenous to Norway, these musical imports gradually became Norwegian in character as they were influenced by the ornamentation, bowing style, and rhythmic swing typical of the "native" repertoire. For example, the old springdans rubbed off a little on the masurka, and the reinlender was subtly shaped by the old halling.[14]

Before Ole's family left Norway, they would likely have had opportunities to hear the vals and polka. The vals, a dance in $\frac{3}{4}$ time, was known at least by 1799 in Norway.[15] The polka, a lively dance in $\frac{2}{4}$ time, was taught by dancing masters in Norway by the 1830s.[16] Ole's family might not have heard the reinlender before immigrating, since it seems to have arrived in Norway during the 1860s.[17] The reinlender, another dance in $\frac{2}{4}$, is more relaxed than the polka.

These Pan-European dances also spread to America, where they were carried westward by early pioneers of many ethnicities. Here, the corresponding dances were generally known as the waltz, the mazurka, the schottische, and the polka. Waltzes and polkas had certainly reached Minnesota by the 1850s, schottisches and mazurkas a bit later. In the Upper Midwest, these dances proved more adaptable than bygdedans to multiethnic communities. Some of the Norwegian waltzes might have sounded a bit unusual to the German neighbors but certainly not enough to discourage them from dancing to them.[18] For unknown reasons, Ole collected no mazurkas. However, the other tune types are all represented in the tunebook, roughly in proportion to their relative popularity in Minnesota as noted by the folklorist Philip Nusbaum: twenty waltzes, eleven reinlenders and schottisches, and ten polkas.[19]

While Scandinavian Americans have come to use the terms reinlender and schottische more or less interchangeably, a closer look at these tunes in Ole's collection reveals some distinguishing features. The reinlenders (tunes #26, #37, #38, #49, and #64) exhibit characteristics typical of that genre found in nineteenth-century Norwegian manuscripts, such as the Stulen and Jevnager notebooks in the collections of the National Library of Norway.[20] Notated in $\frac{2}{4}$ time, they are usually three-part tunes with key changes in each part. Their phrase structure is modular in that each four-measure phrase is generally organized into distinct two-measure units, each featuring a particular melodic sequence or rhythmic motif. The musical idea in each of these two-measure units is often somewhat self-contained.

By contrast, Ole's schottisches (tunes #44, #54, #57, #69, #70, and #81), most of which appear to have been composed later than the reinlenders, are generally written in $\frac{4}{4}$ time, are three- or four-part tunes (also with frequent key changes), and have a freer melodic structure. A musical idea may stretch beyond the two-measure unit (see, e.g., the first four measures of #54). Some of the schottisches (see #54 and #57) have English-language titles and feature arpeggiation similar to hornpipe melodies in published American anthologies of fiddle tunes.

Why make these distinctions, given that the same basic dance is usually performed today, whether the tune is called a reinlender or a schottische? One reason is that a designation of reinlender or schottische in Ole's tunebook is a clue to the origin of each example. All of Ole's reinlenders can be traced back to Norway, with the possible exception of the untitled #26, whose exact origin remains unknown to me. In contrast, it seems likely that many of the schottisches Ole collected either originated in America or were brought here, not necessarily by Norwegian musicians. The origin of these tunes is worth noting because distinct variants of the dance developed in different countries. In Norway, some of these include the *byte reinlender*, in which the dancers switch partners after each round of turns; reinlenders with multiple figures, such as the *gammel reinlender* and the Sunnmøre reinlender; the *firkantreinlender* for two couples; the *stabberinglender*, and local variants such as the *Rørosringlender*.[21] The schottische certainly evolved over time in American ballrooms. One late nineteenth-century dance manual describes five different variations on the schottische.[22] One of these American variations, the military schottische, sometimes called the barn dance, is thought to have influenced the form of the schottische popular today in Scandinavia and in Scandinavian American communities, in which the partners begin the dance standing side by side.[23] Examples of published music for the military schottische from the 1880s and 1890s can be found in American sheet music repositories. The melodies of #69 and #81 in Ole's collection are typical of these popular American schottisches.

Storgårdsmusikk

Within the gammaldans repertoire of Ole's manuscript, violinistic tunes and connections to Hedmark in eastern Norway are plentiful. Many of the waltzes, reinlenders, and polkas in the collection are characteristic of a genre known as *storgårdsmusikk*, a type of ensemble music that was played on wealthy farming estates in the flatland areas of Hedmark during the nineteenth century. The area surrounding Lake Mjøsa (Norway's largest lake), including neighboring districts in Oppland and Akershus, was a major center for the development of this music. As a sort of high-style gammaldans music for the ballroom, Atle Lien Jenssen described it as "dance music in art style."[24] It featured the regular fiddle. Ole seems to have greatly admired this repertoire, judging from some typical examples in his tunebook: tunes #32–34 (three polkas), #37 (reinlender), and #39 and #53 (waltzes).

During the heyday of storgårdsmusikk, several well-known fiddler-composers led orchestras that traveled around Hedmark, sometimes by way of Lake Mjøsa, and played for dances on the big farming estates. Instrumentation varied, but the larger ensembles included first and second violin, cello, clarinet, cornet, piano, and string bass.[25] Many of the musicians had formal training and played from scored arrangements; others played by ear and improvised harmony lines on the spot.[26]

This was music for upper-class environments. It was not the traditional music that would have been played at that time in the homes of husmenn or laborers.[27] Although storgårdsmusikk was influenced by European art music, especially by Viennese ballroom music, it did grow into something uniquely Norwegian. Clearly, these fiddler-composers drew inspiration from their home areas. Place names and other local references appear frequently in the titles for their compositions, in the words of Alan Jabbour, "conveying through the fiddler's repertoire, publicly announced, a celebration of sense of place and way of life."[28] Early folk music collectors were not eager to document storgårdsmusikk because it did not represent the oldest traditional music from the area. However, the genre emerged as a distinctive mode of performance, and its foremost composers left a treasure of old dance music that was a typical product of the encounter between village and city. Its roots were in the traditional fiddler's music, but the form was adapted to the ballroom and arranged for large groups of stringed instruments.[29] Probably only a handful of tunes from the storgårdsmusikk genre ever passed into oral tradition, but the music has survived in a substantial number of notebooks from musicians of the era. In recent years, ensembles in Norway such as Hollos Efterfølgere and Over Stok og Steen have been reviving this repertoire, recording it, and playing it at dances and festivals.

The following section lists some of the composers of this genre who are represented in Ole Hendricks's tunebook.

From Balstad to Bakstad

Three tunes in Ole's tunebook (#33, Polka; #41, Polka; and #63, Vals) are attributed to one of the earliest of these ensemble leaders in Hedmark, Hans P. Balstad (1815–58). Balstad came from Nes, now part of Ringsaker on the eastern shore of Mjøsa. His renowned ensemble, Balstad-musikken, consisted of three fiddlers (including Hans's older brother Thor, also an accomplished fiddler), clarinet, and bass. The ensemble was active on both sides of the lake, traveling often to the western (Oppland) shore to perform in the Toten area. Like Ole Hendricks, Hans Balstad was a farmer, but music was his true calling. When Hans died at the age of forty-three, his brother Thor took over as ensemble leader.[30] Sometime after 1865, Thor emigrated to Cato, near Manitowoc in eastern Wisconsin.[31]

All three attributions to Balstad are in Ole's own handwriting. I have been unable to confirm two of these attributions by locating them in other collections; however, the third tune (#41, Polka) is actually *not* from Balstad. It comes from another source altogether, some forty-five miles farther south:

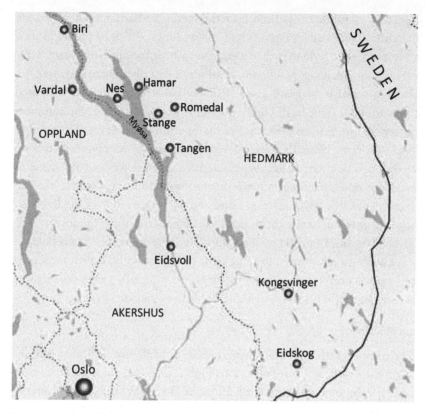

Figure 19. Map of area surrounding Lake Mjøsa in eastern Norway

Hans P. Bakstad (1824–1902) of Eidsvoll on the south end of Lake Mjøsa, in the neighboring county of Akershus. With only one letter's difference in the two names, it is easy to imagine how Ole—or whoever his source was— might have gotten the name confused. The Bakstad family produced several generations of musicians. Hans's father, Peder (Per) Gulbrandsen Bakstad (1768–1864), played for dances in Stange and Romedal in Hedmark and traveled frequently to Oslo for orchestral work before settling in Eidsvoll in 1824. There he established an orchestra that played for dances in the area. His son Hans, often called "Bakstakken," became the foremost musician in Eidsvoll. Hans played bass and cello in his father's ensemble but was better known as a fiddler and clarinetist. He also played the lur, a horn made of wood and traditionally wrapped in birch bark.[32] Hans had an extensive repertoire of fiddle tunes from his father and grandfather, including more than fifty traditional springdans and halling tunes, which he played in such an idiosyncratic style that they were said to be impossible to notate. Ludvig Lindemann, an early folk music collector, described them as having "an amazing number of grace notes."[33] Hans Bakstad apparently composed tunes, too, but since he did not write music himself, many of the compositions were lost. Fortunately, some of his repertoire was captured by another local musician, Hans Borgersen (1862–1947), whose notebooks contain a version of Ole's #41, Polka. Whether Bakstakken composed this tune or handed it down from his father is open to speculation. Of course, the fact that one of Ole's "Balstad" tunes turns out to be from one of the Bakstads begs the question of whether a Bakstad is the source of the other two "Balstad" tunes, but I have so far been unable to determine this. Hans Bakstad was known to play with a joy and vigor that infected his fellow musicians and made a deep impression on listeners. It is especially sad to note that he gave up music in his later years due to his son's pietistic attitude.[34]

Lars Hollo

The composer of #59, Waltz—*Björneblaken*, while not indicated in Ole's manuscript, can be identified as Lars Hollo (1826–98), another prominent fiddler, composer, and ensemble leader in Hedmark. Lars Hollo came to Hedmark in his early twenties when his family moved from Oppland to a place not far from Nes called Midt-Hollostuen (from which the name Hollo comes). Theirs was a musical family, and Lars had his first violin lessons from his father. Before long, he was a member of the orchestra his father directed. For a short time, Lars played the flute in Hans Balstad's ensemble until he, Lars, bought a house in Hamar, where he lived for the rest of his life. He was a quiet, steady man who worked at the local teacher training college, taught violin students, and led a famous ensemble that played for dances all over Hedmark. This ensemble consisted of first and second violin, cornet, clarinet, double bass, and piano. Hollo composed dance music and arranged it for this ensemble. Many of Hollo's notebooks and arrangements survive and are described by Lien Jenssen, who speculates that had Hollo an opportunity to pursue serious musical study, his abilities might have stretched beyond the composition of dance music. In any case, his lyrical melodies and his orchestra were much loved locally. Lien Jenssen also notes that

Hollo's music is rife with technical challenges, and the first violin part (which Hollo himself would have played) requires well-developed technique.[35]

Anders Sørensen

The most famous of the Hedmark fiddler-composers, Anders Sørensen (1821–96), is represented in Ole's collection by at least three tunes. From humble origins on a croft in Romedal, Sørensen left for Oslo as a teenager to pursue a career in classical music. In addition to mastering the horn[36] and cello, Sørensen was a brilliant violinist and, very briefly, a student of the celebrated Ole Bull. Many anecdotes reveal that Sørensen was also a prideful man, prone to mood swings, by turns impatient and generous, and had a serious alcohol addiction. By 1860 his wife had left him, disappearing to America along with their two daughters, and Sørensen returned to Hedmark. From then on, he lived as an itinerant musician, performing as a soloist or sometimes in a duet with another fiddler but never as the leader of an orchestra. He had many fiddle students and a reputation as an exacting teacher. He occasionally traveled as far away as Stockholm or Copenhagen but always returned to Hedmark. Relying completely on the hospitality of others, he never owned much more than his instrument and the clothes on his back. Nevertheless, he had many friends and was apparently a consummate performer not only of his own compositions but also concert pieces by Edvard Grieg, Ole Bull, and others. His playing was emotionally affecting, and people traveled long distances to hear him.[37]

One source of income for Sørensen was the composition of tunes dedicated to certain benefactors. In all, he composed at least forty-four tunes, many of them gems of the dance repertoire. At least two of them—*Den ubemærkte*, often called Sørensen's Waltz, and *En Hilsen til Hamar*, often called Sørensen's Reinlender—became part of the oral tradition and were later popularized in America through published collections. However, Lars Gunhildsberg (1916–87), who searched relentlessly for Sørensen manuscripts and collected extensive oral history concerning him, concluded that many of Sørensen's compositions had been lost.[38]

A total of nine tunes in Ole's collection are attributed to Sørensen. Not all of these attributions are in Ole's handwriting. I have been able to confirm only two of these attributions (#71, *Hilsen til Födehjemmet*, which Ole titled Bergens Vals, and #83, *Den ubemærkte*, titled "Vals of Sörnsen" in the manuscript). In addition, #72, Fandango (to be discussed in more detail later) was composed, or perhaps arranged, by Sørensen. I was not able to establish any definite connection between Sørensen and the other six tunes. However, Thomas Nilssen, of Løten, Norway, who has deep knowledge of musical traditions in Hedmark, notes that the style of #39, Waltz of Spand Berg–Brudens Sorg, is consistent with Sørensen.[39] It is certainly possible that some of Sørensen's "lost tunes" have been preserved in obscure tune-books on the other side of the Atlantic.

Martinus Nielsen Spangberg

Spangberg, variously spelled, is another name that crops up in Ole's manuscript (see #39, Waltz of Spand Berg–Brudens Sorg, attributed to Anders Sørensen; #62, Waltz of M. Spangberg; and #63, Vals attributed to Hans Balstad, which includes the notation "Spenberg #4").

Again, these attributions to Sørensen and Balstad are unconfirmed. Sifting through various pieces of evidence, I surmise that these tunes were probably associated with Martinus Nielsen Spangberg (1829–98), an ensemble leader from Stange (located on the east side of Lake Mjøsa, just south of Hamar); his ensemble, Spangbergsmusikken, was known to perform in the big dance halls in Hamar.[40] In addition, the name Spangberg appears in manuscripts of Hamar's Lars Hollo.[41] Whether Spangberg actually composed the tunes that Ole collected is uncertain, but it seems quite likely they came from Spangberg's repertoire.

Figure 20. Ole's attribution of this waltz to "M. Spangberg" suggests an association with Martinus Nielsen Spangberg. From page [64] of the tunebook. Courtesy of Beth Hoven Rotto.

Few details about Spangberg's musical life are presently available, but he was apparently a very active musician, well-known as a conductor and the director of one of the early men's choirs in Hamar: the singing association affiliated with the Hamar Håndverkerforening (the local association of craftsmen).[42] After being apprenticed to a painter in Hamar as a young man, in 1867 Spangberg purchased a farm in Stange called Sveen. He seems to have been successful financially. By 1886 he also owned properties named Sveplassene and Bekkehagen, and these farms remained in the family at least until the 1950s.[43] Spangberg was also an accountant for the Atlungstad distillery nearby.

D. O. Wold

A less well-known but possibly more influential Hedmark musician represented in the manuscript is Dyre Olssen Vold (D. O. Wold, 1830–1912), who, like Spangberg, was a native of Stange. The name Vold comes from Friisvold, the farm outside Stange where his family lived.[44] According to parish records, Wold played the waldhorn in a military band.[45] He was also a violinist and a composer of tunes.[46] Wold is particularly interesting because in 1868 he immigrated to Black River Falls, Wisconsin, only forty miles from where Ole's family lived in Portland.[47] Since Wold arrived in Wisconsin well before Ole left for Dakota Territory, it is likely that Ole knew of Wold. Furthermore, an early map shows a road running south from Black River Falls and which appears to have passed near Portland.[48] Had D. O. Wold ever had occasion to travel to La Crosse, Portland may have been on his route. According to his obituary, Wold was "one of the finest violinists who ever resided in this section. When he first came here he was quite popular in giving parlor concerts on his violin and will be well remembered by old settlers. . . . He was also in demand as an instructor on the violin."[49] It is conceivable, but not certain, that Ole received his initial training on the fiddle from Wold, and with it the appreciation of Hedmark style and tunes evident in the tunebook.

At some point Wold retired from public performing and played only at home. He seems to have been a man of many talents and the subject of colorful anecdotes. His obituary mentions that he was "a painter by trade" and "an artist as a painter," leaving one to wonder whether he painted houses or portraits. One of his descendants claims that he was a "Musician,

Band Leader, Fiddler, Phrenologist, Dairy Farmer."[50] Thomas Nilssen mentioned that according to some stories, Wold is said to have played with Ole Bull.[51]

D. O. Wold is the source of two appealing tunes in Ole's collection: #37, Reinlender, and #66, Polka. Ole's notation at the end of the polka ("Elbow Lake, Minnesota") led me to wonder whether Wold ever lived in Elbow Lake, but I have not found his name in local records. One can imagine, though, that Wold might have visited Elbow Lake, at the invitation of relatives or by Ole himself.

Tunes from Other Hedmark Sources

Several of Ole's tunes have less definite Hedmark connections. For example, #74, Klingenberg Polka, was also collected by Nils T. Midtlien (1875–1943) of Lismarka, Hedmark (see "The Transcriptions" in Part 2). Another example is #49, Reinlender, which also appears in a manuscript of Edvard Andresen (1849–1929). Andresen, a fiddler, lived near Tangen on the east side of Lake Mjøsa, south of Stange. He assembled two notebooks of music, and since he was originally from Eidsvoll, he probably had some music from Hans Bakstad.[52]

Figure 21. Reinlender by D. O. Wold on page [37] of Ole's manuscript. Courtesy of Beth Hoven Rotto.

Turdanser

The balls at the large farming estates where storgårdsmusikk was played also included some older dances from a genre called *turdanser* (figure dance).[53] These dances involved several "tours" (parts or figures) in which a particular number of couples moved to somewhat complicated choreography that closely followed the music. Different versions of these figure dances were also practiced in other parts of Norway. Ole's collection includes two examples of turdanser, the previously mentioned fandango (#72) and a figaro (#73).

The Norwegian fandango, unrelated to the Spanish one, was very popular in Hedmark from about 1820 to 1900. It had two sections in duple meter and one in triple meter. Because it was long and was danced at a brisk pace, it favored the young and energetic dancer.[54] Klara Semb, who documented many of the older dances, stated that if there were many guests at a ball, a complete fandango could take an hour or more, and she knew of an instance where it took over two hours.[55] Semb collected versions of the fandango that were danced in Østlandet in eastern Norway and Namdalen in central Norway.[56] The origin of the fandango in Ole's manuscript is unclear. Ole attributed it to "Bergirsen," but Lars Gunhildsberg, who conducted exhaustive research, believed it was a composition of Anders Sørensen (see "The Transcriptions" in Part 2).

Another type of turdanser represented in the tunebook is the figaro. One of the more courtly dances, it progressed at a slower, dignified tempo and featured sweeping bows and curtsies. Three different versions evolved: the *figaro med en mølle* (figaro with one "mill" or square), *figaro med to møller* (figaro with two mills), and *figaro der alle dansar* (figaro where everyone dances).[57] According to Semb, it was the first dance after the meal was served, when the dancers were in good spirits after their repast. It was danced by people of all ages and was popular through World War I.[58] Ole's collection includes a well-known figaro melody composed by Niels Christian Brøgger (1783–1827). Brøgger was a soloist and music teacher on the nascent classical music scene in Christiania (now Oslo) in the early years of the nineteenth century. Like Anders Sørensen and D. O. Wold, Brøgger played the horn.[59] He was apparently quite talented but never achieved real prominence, perhaps due to his choice of instrument. At that time, the violin or piano were preferred by upwardly mobile musical artists. Brogger's later years were spent in the coastal city of Christianssand (now Kristiansand), where he died at the age of forty-three.[60]

Why Hedmark?

All of this begs the question of how storgårdsmusikk came to be so well represented in the repertoire of a *telemarking*. It seems certain that Ole did not find this repertoire in published sources during his most active years.[61] That he knew fiddlers who came from this region of Norway is a distinct possibility. During his youth in Wisconsin, several towns in La Crosse County (including Holmen, Onalaska, Stevenstown, and West Salem—all

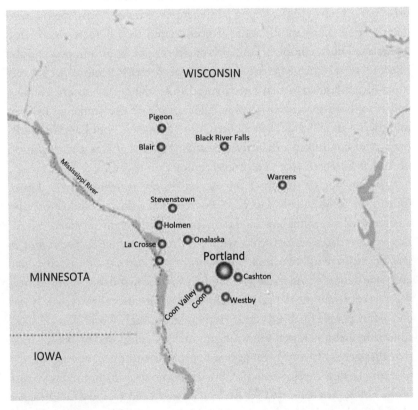

Figure 22. Map of southwestern Wisconsin, showing some communities settled by people from Hedmark, Oppland, or Akershus in Norway.

within about thirty miles of Portland) had significant concentrations of immigrants from Hedmark. Many of these immigrants would have passed through Monroe County on their way to and from La Crosse. As mentioned earlier, ensembles from Nes and Hamar, for example, played for dances on both sides of Lake Mjøsa, so this style of music was known in parts of Oppland and Akershus as well. Pockets of immigrants from Oppland and Akershus also existed near Portland.[62]

The proximity of D. O. Wold has already been noted, and he could certainly have been the source of the Spangberg tunes. Even closer than Wold was Anton Tømten (1855–1927), who lived in Coon, near Westby, Wisconsin, about ten miles from Ole's family in Portland. Tømten came from Biri, on the Oppland side of Lake Mjøsa. Before emigrating with his family in 1868, the young Anton probably grew up hearing this music and thus carried it with him to America. He became well known around Westby as "Spelemann [Fiddler] Tomten," and since he was known to walk as far as twenty miles to play for a dance, it would be surprising if the two young fiddlers, almost neighbors, had not met and even played together.[63] A bit farther away was the town of Blair, about sixty miles distant, where many fiddlers from Solør in southern Hedmark settled.[64] Hans Olson Samuelstad (1841–92), a fiddler from Vardal, Oppland, on the western shore of Lake Mjøsa, settled in Pigeon in Trempealeau County, about sixty miles from Portland.[65] Even if Ole did not know Anton Tømten, Wold, or Samuelstad personally, they might have had musical acquaintances in common. Given the flood of immigrants and the difficulty of tracing individual fiddlers, it is safe to assume that my list of fiddlers is far from complete. Manuscript collections of tunes most probably circulated among musicians eager to learn new repertoire, and tunes were often copied from one musician's notebook to another. Moreover, Ole no doubt had opportunities to learn tunes by ear from other fiddlers in the area.

After Ole left Wisconsin, communities of people from Hedmark and Oppland would not have been too far from his homes in Walcott and Elbow Lake. Hedmark was strongly represented in the towns of Dwight and Ransom (about twenty-five and forty-five miles from Walcott, respectively). Among the residents of Elbow Lake were immigrants from Stange, Eidskog, and Kongsvinger in Hedmark. Ensemble music of the *storgård* variety was

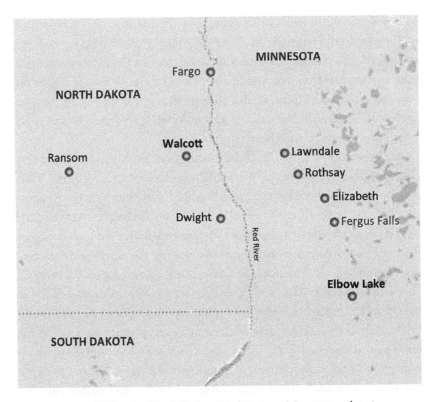

Figure 23. Map of eastern North Dakota and western Minnesota, showing some communities settled by people from Hedmark, Oppland, or Akershus in Norway.

performed in all of these districts.[66] Additional pockets of immigrants from Hedmark or Oppland lay within fifty miles of Elbow Lake, in the towns of Elizabeth, Lawndale, and Rothsay in Ottertail County.[67] Rothsay even had Lutheran congregations named Hedemarken and Hamar. In fact, Ottertail County was home to one of the largest concentrations of immigrants from Stange, as more than twenty families settled there.[68] Again, Ole could have come into contact with musicians from any of these communities during his Elbow Lake years. In addition, Ole occasionally traveled to Minneapolis, and it is possible that on one of these trips he met Andreas Torsen Tomta (1828–1912), a prominent fiddler from Vinger in southern Hedmark who immigrated to Minneapolis in 1881.[69]

AMERICAN INFLUENCES

Quadrilles

Ole's Norwegian repertoire—the gammaldans, storgårdsmusikk, and turdanser tunes—suggests that he had a strong sense of a shared Norwegian
heritage, rather than just being closely identified with the music of his
home district in Telemark. Nusbaum has remarked that this was characteristic of many Norwegians in Minnesota.[70] Although Ole was a first-
generation immigrant, he came to this country at a young age and would
have adapted to the surrounding culture with greater ease. He seems to
have had an awareness of being part of an American community that included people of other backgrounds, and he would do his best to keep
them all moving on the dance floor.

It is not surprising, then, that his tunebook contains music for quadrilles,
another transplanted European dance form that was popular in ballrooms
all over America from about 1820 through the end of the century.[71] In
Minnesota, quadrilles were danced at least from the 1850s.[72] I suspect that
Ole's quadrille tunes came from American sources; however, the quadrille
form (*kvadrilje*) was also danced in Norway, where it was part of the turdanser genre. In Norway, the quadrille's popularity dates from the late eighteenth century through the middle of the nineteenth century.[73]

As in modern square dancing, for a quadrille a set of four couples formed
a square. Each couple faced the center from the four sides of the square and
danced only with the other three couples in the set. Many nineteenth-
century dance manuals provide directions for various types of quadrilles.[74]
In its original form, the entire dance consisted of five figures, separated by
brief pauses, with each figure being danced to a lively tune in $\frac{2}{4}$ or $\frac{6}{8}$ time.
Ole's tunebook includes twenty-three quadrille sets and eight additional
quadrille tunes. A few of these tunes (apparently his favorites) are repeated,
being recombined into new sets. This fact suggests that he might sometimes have read from the tunebook during dances, with some tunes in a
new set recopied to minimize page turns.

None of Ole's quadrille sets include five tunes, however. Nineteen of these
sets consist of three tunes, and two consist of four tunes. Thus, it appears
that in Elbow Lake, as in many communities by that time, shorter quadrille
sets of three figures were common practice. It all came down to length, it

seems. An 1889 dance manual advises, "The majority of Quadrilles consist of five numbers. As a rule, it is well to omit one, generally No. 4, and dance but four numbers. Otherwise, many Quadrilles would take up too much time."[75] Another manual published the same year states that "at all balls where there is a long list of dances to be got through with, all quadrilles are generally reduced to three figures."[76] In addition, shorter quadrilles of only three or four figures appear in dance manuals from this era.[77] The third and last figure of a quadrille was typically danced to a tune in quick $\frac{2}{4}$, often a reel or breakdown (tunes #1c, #9c, #16c, #17c, and #19c in Ole's collection are good examples).[78]

Near the end of the nineteenth century, the quadrille began to go out of style, except among older people who continued to enjoy this "stately" dance.[79] Waltzes and two-steps were becoming more popular, especially among younger people in more urban areas. An 1898 account in the *Minneapolis Tribune* reflects these changing tastes: "A program of two-steps and waltzes . . . contained lancers [a variety of quadrille] and quadrilles in the opening half in deference to the taste of the [older] chaperones."[80] However, quadrilles continued to be danced in rural areas for several decades. Folios that included music for three-figure quadrilles were issued by publishers such as M. M. Cole in Chicago at least through the 1930s.[81] Leonard Finseth (1911–91), the well-known Norwegian American fiddler of Mondovi, Wisconsin, played a number of quadrille tunes. By Finseth's time, these were often played as standalone tunes, independent of any set.[82]

Most of Ole's quadrilles, even the few with more distinctive names, proved impossible to trace during this study, given the resources and time available. During his active years, many collections containing tunes for quadrilles were published by Elias Howe in Boston, J. W. Pepper in Philadelphia, E. T. Root in Chicago, and others, often printed on poor-quality paper that has not survived. These collections were advertised in newspapers, and some could even be ordered through Sears Roebuck. Ole could have gleaned tunes from any number of collections, although he does not seem to have gotten them from any published by Howe. Quadrille tunes, sometimes referred to by the older term *cotillion*, also exist in many vernacular (but not indexed) music manuscripts. The wealth of published and manuscript collections aside, Ole might well have acquired some of these tunes aurally, and three of the tunes came from a source close to home: his friend Swen Olson.

Fiddle Tunes

The remainder of Ole's collection is solidly American. He collected a few Anglo-Celtic fiddle tunes that had been included in many published tune collections and were common in oral tradition across the country. These include a number of standard hornpipes, such as #22, College Hornpipe. The hornpipe was a popular theatrical dance from the late eighteenth century and into the nineteenth century. Today, many old-time fiddlers play these tunes as reels, but according to Howard Marshall, "until the end of the [nineteenth] century, a hornpipe was . . . an energetic, dotted-time solo-step dance" performed by athletic dancers at places like tent shows and circuses.[83] Ole might have found these tunes in the monolithic tune anthologies published by Elias Howe, such as *The Musician's Companion* series or *Ryan's Mammoth Collection,* since Ole's versions are similar to these published versions.

Minstrel Tunes

One American musical phenomenon that surfaces in Ole's tunebook is minstrelsy. The minstrel show, which became America's most popular form of stage entertainment by the 1840s, featured white performers who blacked their faces and performed songs and skits that parodied the Southern plantation slave. The minstrel show was, of course, inherently racist. As summed up by Christopher Martin, "These minstrel shows appropriated— and often caricatured—African American performance traditions, relied on athleticism and verbal wordplay, and created a variety of enduring, and vicious, racial stereotypes."[84] However, the syncopated rhythms characteristic of minstrel songs and banjo playing would have a profound influence on American popular music, jazz, and contemporary folk music.

After the Civil War, black minstrel troupes came to prominence, showcasing the talents of African American performers.[85] By the time Ole lived in Elbow Lake, the zenith of minstrelsy was past, but touring minstrel troupes, such as Lew Johnson's Minstrels, came through town and performed at Olson and Hendricks's hall.[86] Johnson was the most successful black owner/manager of African American minstrel troupes. He specialized in organizing tours to smaller, rural places where there was less competition from white-owned minstrel troupes.[87] Elbow Lake would have been in

Johnson's target market. Other troupes that came through town included Alexander's Plantation[88] and the Concordia Negro Concert Co. (featuring Shine, the "Norwegian negro").[89] Minstrel shows continued to be performed in smaller towns across the United States until well into the twentieth century.

Three tunes in Ole's manuscript—#30, Darkie's Dream; #31, Whistling Coon; and #45, Buck and Wing Dance—come from the minstrel tradition or its post–Civil War offshoot, vaudeville. Ole might have played them at the minstrel show put on by the locals at Olson and Hendricks's hall in Elbow Lake on February 28, 1895.[90] At least on paper, Ole's versions of these tunes are quite straight, lacking much in the way of the syncopation typical of this music. To judge by his tunebook, minstrel tunes were obviously not Ole's usual offering, but the sponsors of the event later expressed their "hearty thanks . . . [to] all who participated in the minstrel show . . . especially to Mr. Ole Hendricks for his untiring energy in providing such excellent music."[91]

Music from American Publications

Ole collected a few of his tunes from sheet music or popular published arrangements of his era. For example, #79, 6th Lancers–Annette, came from an edition published by J. W. Pepper in Philadelphia. Similarly, #80, Life Is a Dream Waltz, composed by Friedrich Zikoff, was available from various American publishers including Oliver Ditson. Ole's daughter Clara was an able pianist; one imagines that some of these tunes came from music in her piano bench. Since Ole participated in brass bands in the area, band music might have been another source of material.

COMPARISON TO OTHER TUNE COLLECTIONS

As we have seen, Ole's Norwegian repertoire is unusual in that it was not from his home county of Telemark. Had he never immigrated, he probably would have had a quite different repertoire. While researching composers named in the manuscript, I examined a variety of tunebooks dating from the nineteenth/early twentieth century that have been digitized by the National Library of Norway. The more "Norwegian" portions of Ole's collection are similar to other manuscripts from eastern Norway (e.g., Severin Jevnager and John Stulen notebooks)[92] in general melodic style and structure, and in notational conventions. These manuscripts are rich in waltzes, polkas, and reinlenders, many composed by Balstad, Hollo, Sørensen, and others. However, they also contain some older tune types not represented in Ole's collection, such as *englis, feier, firetur, menuett, polonaise*, and *varsovienne*, as well as the occasional older traditional tune, such as a springdans. By contrast, Ole drew from music sources popular after about 1850.

The only comparable manuscript by a Norwegian American that was available to me for comparison was one compiled a generation earlier by Johan Arndt (Mostad) (1833–1909). Arndt, who immigrated from Trøndelag in Norway to Winneshiek County, Iowa, also collected waltzes, polkas, schottisches, and hornpipes. Additionally, he collected several other types of Norwegian tunes, including mazurkas, marches, several types of tunes in the polka family not represented in Ole's collection (gallops, hamborgers, gallopades, and hopvalses), and traditional springdans melodies. Arndt collected no quadrille tunes but did collect a similar genre: cotillions. Unlike Ole, he collected no reinlenders, turdanser, or storgårdsmusikk.[93] Arndt's manuscript is voluminous, and I did not attempt a tune-by-tune comparison, but I note that Arndt collected another version of Ole's #70, Schottische Crescent.

Curiously, one finds very little overlap between Ole's collection and the 166 tunes collected by LeRoy Larson in his "Scandinavian-American Folk Dance Music of the Norwegians in Minnesota." Unless some tune variants have escaped my attention, the only tune in both collections is Anders Sørensen's *Den ubemærkte*. The transformation of the violinistic *Den ubemærkte* in Ole's collection (#83) to the fiddle-friendly versions in Larson (#64 and #155) shows a prime example of the forces of communal re-creation at work. Perhaps the two collections lack additional overlap because three-quarters of Larson's source musicians were born in 1900 or later; all were at least thirty years younger than Ole. Many were born in Minnesota and had parents or grandparents who had come from various areas of Norway. A few had Swedish roots. Most had grown up listening to the radio and 78 rpm records. By then, the accordion was having a strong influence on the music. Larson did field work in many areas of the state; he considered most of the tunes as belonging to "rather isolated rural 'pockets.'" Further, he observed that "two fiddlers who lived only a few miles apart would know tunes that were unfamiliar to each other."[94] Robert Andresen noticed something similar: "Among Swedish fiddlers there seemed to have been a core of best-loved tunes known to all fiddlers, but the tradition among Norwegian and Norwegian-American fiddlers usually is that each must have his personal collection of tunes, distinct from other fiddlers."[95] Of course, at least a portion of the tunes Larson collected were alive in the oral tradition, and Ole might have known some of them well enough that he did not bother to write them down. Interestingly, musical literacy does not seem to have been common among Larson's informants, aural transmission being more usual.

One striking difference between Larson's and Ole's collections is the wealth of tunes collected by Ole that have three or more parts. Even if we exclude his quadrilles, hornpipes, and minstrel tunes, the remaining tunes with three or more parts account for about 31 percent of Ole's collection, compared to about 19 percent of Larson's collection. That subset of Ole's tunebook includes seventeen three-part tunes, eleven four-part tunes, and eleven tunes with five or more parts. Another difference between the two collections is the higher range of many of Ole's tunes. While Larson's fiddle-playing sources contributed only six tunes ranging as high as D or E above the treble staff, the tunes in Ole's collection require much more position work.

In Janet Kvam's 1986 follow-up study, "Norwegian-American Dance Music in Minnesota and Its Roots in Norway: A Comparative Study," she sought to discover how much of Larson's collection actually came from Norway, and whether musicians in Norway recognized any of it. As it turned out, Kvam's "panel of experts" did recognize more than half of the tunes, and some of their remarks are interesting in relation to Ole's tunebook. Atle Lien Jenssen, whose writings have been cited (see nn. 24, 26, 27) in connection with Hedmark, mentioned that many of Larson's tunes were popularized on 78 rpm records. (Ole's collection predates the ethnic recording boom that occurred from 1910 to 1930.) Ottar Akre from Hedmark surmised that Larson's source musicians probably learned by ear rather than from written music, whereas Ole absorbed at least some of his repertoire through written sources. Other musicians Kvam consulted seemed to have different perceptions about whether Larson's collection owed much to the music of Hedmark that Ole so admired. Erling Sjøk, of Garmo in

Gudbrandsdal, observed that "many melodies in [Larson's] collection remind him of two flatland fiddlers' styles: Lars Hollo and Severin [Jevnager]."[96] Ånon Egeland from Oslo had a similar impression: "Many of the melodies are 'flatland' style, which is the style of the flat farm districts in eastern Norway."[97] In contrast, Terje Bronken of Vågåmo in Gudbrandsdal observed that "the best melodies were the ones used in the dances at the big farms where wealthier Norwegians lived," and he was puzzled why these melodies were not more prevalent in Larson's collection.[98]

I checked some recent collections of Norwegian American music from Minnesota and Wisconsin, both print and recorded, without finding that any of them included anything from Ole's repertoire. I found none of his tunes in the classic 1980s LPs *Tunes from the Amerika Trunk* and *Norwegian-American Music from Minnesota*.[99] Nor did I find any of his tunes in Mary Pat Kleven's anthology of repertoire from Elmo Wick (1924–2009). Wick was born in Sunburg, Minnesota, approximately sixty-five miles from Elbow Lake, to a family with roots in Hallingdal, a valley in Buskerud, Norway. As a fiddler, Wick was comfortable playing in higher positions on the fingerboard, to judge by several tunes that extend to high E. Larson's report of largely aural transmission is born out in Kleven's remark that "in his later years, Elmo . . . learned how to read and write music. Up to that point, he and his family and neighbors all learned and played tunes by ear."[100] A more thorough comparison to repertoire of other musicians in the region—such as Leonard Finseth and Johan Arndt—would be a challenging but potentially fascinating follow-up study to the present volume.

A MIXED GROUND

As I thought more about this mysterious tunebook, with its gammaldans tunes and its elaborate composed melodies, I wondered, "Is this actually folk music?" In Norway, until more recently, the term *folkemusikk* was reserved for bygdedans, the older traditional repertoire that accompanied dances such as the springar, halling, and gangar, whether played on the Hardanger or the regular fiddle. Gammaldans was viewed as a type of popular music, a newer, foreign import, even though musicians in Norway (including some players of the Hardanger fiddle) put their stamp on it. Over the past thirty years, however, gammaldans has been integrated into the folk music scene in Norway.[101] To most Americans, this music—whether played by Norwegians or Norwegian Americans—sounds "ethnic" and, by extension, like folk music. When Ole played gammaldans and storgårds-musik, he played it in typical folk music contexts: rural community dances, barn dances, and house parties; he spent his entire life in rural communities, apart from brief stints in Minneapolis during the 1920s. The written tradition was not his sole source of repertoire. While it is difficult to trace the origins of all the tunes in the tunebook, a portion of them certainly existed in oral tradition. Moreover, whatever musical training Ole managed to obtain would not have been as systematic and formalized as would be sought by a musician aspiring to a professional career in cultivated music.

As a musician, Ole clearly occupied a mixed ground. Not only was he both fiddler and violinist, absorbing repertoire by ear and through notation, but his collection holds both Norwegian and American music. While he was clearly interested in connecting to his heritage through the old-country dance tunes, his eclectic repertoire also included quadrilles, Anglo-Celtic fiddle tunes, minstrel tunes, and waltzes and schottisches that might have come from popular sheet music. Occasionally, a Norwegian tune was interpolated into a set of quadrille tunes (e.g., #8c, Polka). To the traditional music purist, this may sound like degeneration and fragmentation, but those familiar with the work of the folklorist James Leary may recognize the beginnings of the transformative process of creolization.

Creolization occurs when different cultural groups come together and exchange elements of their cultures, resulting in the creation of new expressive forms.[102] As Leary explains, "Upper Midwesterners traded songs and tunes, forging a new regional style that creatively fused their cultural and linguistic similarities and differences."[103] Beginning as early as the 1850s, musicians like Ole Hendricks played repertoires that were accessible to all the listeners and dancers in their ethnically diverse neighborhoods. Succeeding generations would continue to play waltzes, polkas, and schottisches, with the addition of accordions or banjos to the mix, resulting in a distinctive Norwegian American sound. Meanwhile, musicians from the various immigrant groups across the Midwest were learning music from touring performers, radio, recordings, and from each other. By the 1920s, this creolized sound, which owed much to the contributions of Norwegian American musicians, became known as "old-time." By the time Ole died in 1935, this musical genre was beginning to absorb additional elements, like American country and the Hawaiian guitar, resulting in the state of full-blown "pol-kabilly" described in colorful detail by Leary.[104]

The mixed ground Ole occupied was perhaps much more common during his generation than many folk music revivalists today realize. As Robert Andresen observed, "Various forms of music have dramatically influenced each other throughout history. It is foolish to believe totally 'pure' forms exist anywhere. . . . The real story of folk music in [Minnesota and Wisconsin] is probably the story of ethnic music and how that ethnic music evolved here on [America's] northern frontier."[105] Ole Hendricks is certainly part of that story. His storgårdsmusikk repertoire could be seen as yet another manifestation of creolization. Ole took melodies from this light ensemble music played in high-society environments in Norway and integrated those tunes into his hybrid repertoire for the enjoyment of a rural, agrarian audience on the edge of the Great Plains.

CHAPTER THREE

A Farmer and His Fiddle
in the New Century

BACK TO THE LAND

Even as Ole continued to operate the dance hall, he began to turn his attention back to farming. In 1895, he purchased a two-hundred-acre farm about a mile and a half north of Elbow Lake (160 acres were in Sanford Township and another forty acres were located just across the border in Pomme de Terre township).[1] He planned to build a house that spring and move the family to the farm, but apparently they did not vacate the house

№ 288. Bird's Eye View, Elbow Lake, Minn.

Figure 24. View of the town of Elbow Lake from the north, ca. 1908, with Worm Lake (now Flekkefjord Lake) in the distance. Author's collection.

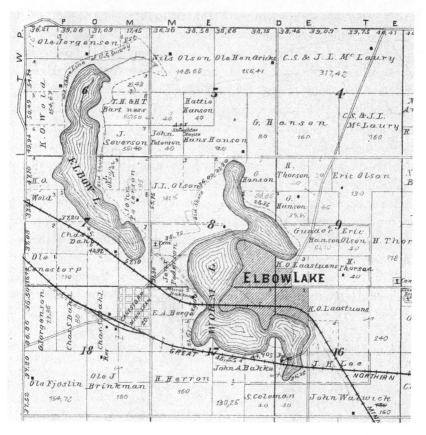

Figure 25. Detail from a 1900 map of Elbow Lake in Grant County, Minnesota. Ole Hendricks's farm can be seen in the top portion. The farm included forty additional acres not pictured on this map. Wheat, oats, rye, barley, flax, buckwheat, corn, and millet were the principal crops in the area; vegetables and small fruits were also grown. Courtesy of the Grant County Historical Society, Elbow Lake, Minnesota.

in town until three years later.[2] In fact, the barn came first. During the summer of 1896 Ole hosted a dance in the new barn that drew a crowd.[3] Later on, he gradually sold off his other properties in town, including his former residence (1899)[4] and "three lots north of Jacob Triese's" (1900).[5]

The family endured some hard times after buying the farm. The nation was in the grip of an economic depression that followed the Panic of 1893. Ole and Elizabeth experienced the deaths of their nine-year-old son Otto

in 1897 and their seven-month-old baby boy in 1901.[6] The drought-prone
Red River Valley went through another dry spell in 1897/98. Wheat leaf
rust destroyed much of the county's wheat crop in 1904; the following year,
wet weather led to a potato blight.[7] Stories that have come down through
the Hendricks family suggest that farming might not have been Ole's strong
suit and that he was happier living in town.[8] However, given the climate,
fluctuations in commodity prices, and price gouging by middlemen and
railroads, many farmers in the region were just a few steps away from ruina-
tion.[9] Barbara Levorsen describes many Norwegian settlers as being "utterly
practical people, wholly devoted to turning seed and toil into money with
which to better their living conditions and, if possible, put something aside
for the time when they could no longer labor. This was neither the time nor
the place for idlers and dreamers."[10] A farmer whose first love was the fiddle might have been regarded by the "utterly practical" as just one more idler.
Yet, like Charles Ingalls's fiddle in the *Little House* saga of struggle to make
a life on the prairie, Ole's fiddle represents something beyond practicality:
"music, spirit, endurance, and a vast repertoire of cultural inheritance."[11]

Figure 26. A threshing crew in Elbow Lake taking a much-needed break during
the wheat harvest, ca. 1906–14. Author's collection.

Perhaps, like the Ingalls family, the Hendrickses might never have "gotten through it all without Pa's fiddle."[12]

The dance hall was in operation at least through July 1899, when the Elbow Lake Union Band gave a concert at "Hendricks' Hall."[13] By that time Ole was apparently no longer owner of the building. In February of that year, the *Grant County News* reported that Schanscke & Honstaf were the new owners of "Ole Hendricks' building on Central avenue next to Skogmo's store."[14] The fact that the town had voted dry in 1896, and again in 1898, might have influenced Ole's decision to sell the building and give up on the saloon business once and for all.

Meanwhile, Ole's children were growing up, and some of them became quite active as singers or instrumentalists. His son Albert (fiddle) and daughter Clara (piano) played with Ole for dances and on concerts sponsored by the Elbow Lake Symphony Club.[15] Albert became very active as a dance musician around the area, forming his own ensemble with Lars Sand.[16]

Even though he no longer owned a dance hall, Ole continued to play for dances in Elbow Lake through 1910. By this time Albert had moved to North Dakota; perhaps Andrew Svien filled his place in the orchestra. After an announcement for a dance at the Opera House to be held on December 3, 1910, the Hendricks Orchestra disappears from the pages of the *Grant County Herald.*[17]

ON TO ISANTI COUNTY

After twenty years in Grant County, Ole had reached a turning point. His brother Halvor moved 180 miles away to St. James, Minnesota, in 1910.[18] In March 1911, having just turned sixty years old, Ole sold his farm.[19] He and his wife moved to a farm in North Branch Township, Isanti County, in eastern Minnesota. The precise reasons for this move are unknown, but there were plenty of things to make a farmer's life difficult in Grant County. During the 1909 harvest, for example, temperatures soared and no less than twenty-seven horses across the county were said to have dropped dead in harness.[20] That same autumn, the area experienced a sudden boom in the grasshopper population, which proceeded to devour the sisal twine used to bind sheaves of harvested wheat.[21] A serious drought followed in 1910.[22] Apparently Ole continued to farm to some extent in Isanti County, but he was growing older. According to census data, his sons Henry and Clarence,

Figure 27. Detail from the 1914 plat map for Isanti County, Minnesota, showing Ole Hendricks's farm in North Branch Township (sections 19 and 20). From the collections of the Minnesota Historical Society.

and sometimes additional laborers, lived and worked on the farm. His other sons Lewis and Olaf lived in the area as well.

Ole seems to have kept a lower profile in Isanti County. He kept up his music—his penchant for fiddling at the fishing hole has already been mentioned—and he may have continued to play for country dances. Larson notes that Scandinavians in certain rural areas of the state continued to dance to the waltz, schottische, and polka for several decades.[23] Nonetheless, Isanti County was not as heavily populated by people of Norwegian background, which might have affected the level of interest in his style of music.[24] If he did play for dances, that fact was not noted by the local newspapers, although a great deal of attention was given to the latest motion pictures and their showtimes. Indeed, the way people spent their leisure time was beginning to change. According to oral history collected by Philip Martin, as automobiles became more ubiquitous, young people could travel farther afield for their entertainment. Those inclined to dance tended to drive to new, larger dance halls and pavilions. These newer, bigger audiences enabled the halls to book professional bands whose repertoire included more popular material.[25] According to advertisements for dances during this period in Isanti County, music was often provided by bands that came up from Minneapolis. One such announcement mentions "traps and xylophone," an instrumentation that suggests that public taste was changing.[26] The larger venues with their crowded dance floors encouraged the use of louder instruments, such as the accordion, whose sound could project even without a sound system. By contrast, a fiddler had to work very hard to be heard.

By World War I, dancing the quadrille, waltz, and polka was out of style, at least among Anglo-American urbanites in places like the Twin Cities. A nostalgic article in the *Minneapolis Sunday Tribune* from 1914 reminisces about the old dances and provides a vivid picture of former times:

"Chasse by your partner and bow-wow-wow! Chasse back and bow-wow again!"

Can't you see it; the narrow, gray-walled hall in the little town; the kerosene lamps emitting the dim light and the strong smell? Oh, that smell of rank kerosene smoke! Even the memory of that smell is almost strong enough to crowd out that of the figure which gave the whole scene vitality, life, soul—the fiddler.

"First couple lead up to the right! Deedle-deedle-dum-tum-dump-tum-dee! Swing once and a half times round! Dum-deedle-dump-tum-dee-dee-dum!"

Can't you feel the floor vibrate under the dancing feet? Can't you see the lamps flicker and almost go out, fanned by the voluminous skirts—18 feet around the bottom if they were an inch—when the boys gave the girls a particular vigorous swing?[27]

Although commercial recordings featuring fiddlers enjoyed a brief heyday during the 1920s, and a younger generation of ethnic old-time music entertainers remained popular through the 1950s, this 1914 account from Minneapolis supports Martin's observation that "increasingly the fiddler was seen in a nostalgic light, a quaint reminder of a time gone by."[28] One manifestation of this nostalgia was the flurry of fiddle contests across the country during the mid- to late 1920s. According to Goertzen, this brief "resurgence of interest in fiddling ... was less a genuine revival than a moment of bold punctuation marking the completion of the shift of fiddling from the center of musical life to the lively but smallish subculture of today."[29]

Originally, the fiddle contests of the 1920s may have been envisioned as a place to showcase the old-time fiddle music of Anglo-Celtic origin. However, in fiddle contests across the Upper Midwest, in places like Fergus Falls, St. Cloud, Albert Lea, and Eau Claire, many fiddlers of Norwegian heritage did very well in the contests, even though their repertoire was not principally Anglo-Celtic. The judges and audiences alike appreciated the Norwegian American brand of old-time fiddling.[30]

One such contest was the Northwest Fiddle Contest held at the State, Garrick, and Lyric Theatres in Minneapolis in early February 1926. At nearly seventy-five, Ole Hendricks entered this competition and made it to the semifinals on the final night—no mean feat, considering his age and the large number of entrants (more than one hundred contestants). This event received extensive coverage in the metro area newspapers, which reported that more than 2,000 people were in the audience for each round, with more than 25,000 people attending throughout the five days of the competition.[31] In fact, the audience acted as jury in this contest, registering their assessment of each fiddler by the volume of their applause. Not surprisingly, showmanship was an element in the competition, and some fiddlers connected with their listeners through the use of humor and trick fiddling skills.

Ole's hometown newspaper reported, "O. A. Hendricks ... was one of the fifteen fiddlers in the final *Minneapolis Tribune*, Finkelstein and Ruben old-time fiddler's contest, held at the State Theatre in Minneapolis last Friday evening. The program was broadcasted over radio station WCCO and many had the privilege of hearing the novel program. The old fiddlers ranged between the ages of 50 and 90. . . . Mr. Hendricks . . . came out about eighth in the final contest, and his many friends in this vicinity congratulate him on his musical ability."[32]

The old dances may have been out of fashion, but clearly Ole could still make the rosin fly!

PART 2

The Tunes, with Annotations

About this Edition

Editorial Conventions

The intent behind this edition is to convey as much information as possible to readers with scholarly interests, while ensuring the transcriptions are also readable by musicians who wish to play this repertoire.

Selection of Tunes

This edition includes all of the tunes in the manuscript, with the following exceptions: duplicate tunes (repeat appearances of individual tunes), fragments or incomplete tunes, and a few of what seem to be harmony lines for unidentified melodies. When a tune appears more than once in the manuscript, only the first instance is printed here, with an indication of where the tune reappears elsewhere in the manuscript.

Tune type	Unique melodies	Additional examples labelled as such within quadrille sets	Transcriptions omitted		
			Duplicates	Incomplete	Harmonies
Quadrille	70	-	4	1	
Waltz	20		1	3	5
Polka	10	1	2	1	
Schottische	6				
Reinlender	5				
Hornpipe	6	1			
Minstrel	3				
Reel or Breakdown	2	2			
Turdanser	2				
Total unique:	**124**				

Figure 28. Number of tunes by tune type.

ORDER OF TUNES

The tunes appear in the same order as in the manuscript, with the exception of the two American Stalwart quadrille tunes, which are not contiguous in the manuscript but are brought together here.

NUMBERING OF TUNES

The numbering is my own. Most of Ole's quadrille sets are groupings of three tunes. All tunes in a particular set have been given the same number, with each tune receiving its own suffix (e.g., 2a, 2b, 2c).

TITLES OF TUNES

In general, Ole's titles are reproduced here as written. For unnamed tunes, a placeholder title (e.g., [Reinlender]) or a title gleaned from other sources, in brackets, has been supplied. Ole's spelling is inconsistent. For ease of referring to particular tunes, I standardized the spelling of quadrille (which sometimes appears as *quadrill*), reinlender (which often appears as *reilander* or *reilender*), schottische, vals (in one instance spelled *wals*), and waltz; in other cases, I supplied additional title words in brackets for clarity. The genealogist Jim Hove explained that during Ole's time, a more relaxed attitude regarding names and spelling prevailed.[1] As revealed in census data, Norwegian was spoken at home while Ole was growing up; however, like many of their generation, neither of his parents could write. Ole would have learned to read and write English in school, and although he spoke Norwegian, he probably would never have been schooled in writing it.

ATTRIBUTIONS

When a composer is named in the manuscript, an effort was made to verify the attribution through comparison to other sources. The phrase "attributed to" in this edition indicates that an attribution could not be confirmed—the tune may indeed be a "lost" tune of that composer, but this is not certain. A composer's name in brackets indicates that it did not appear in the manuscript but was revealed in the course of my research.

FORM OF TUNES

Many tunes contain two *da capo* (repeat from the beginning) markings. These were probably played ABACA, and letters have been supplied to the sections as a visual aid.[2] Where convenient, first and second endings have been added in order to make the note values add up; however, when this more modern practice would have necessitated printing entire sections multiple times, Ole's original section endings were preserved. There is a strong argument that the older practice of placing repeat signs in the middle of a measure, as applied by Ole, is easier to read under pressure (e.g., while playing for dancers). Related to *da capo* and *dal segno* (from the beginning to the sign), Dale Cockrell has observed that "consistency is not a virtue of nineteenth-century notational practice . . . when indicating the precise sections of music to be repeated."[3] Occasionally the form of a tune is unclear from Ole's notation. In these cases, *da capo*, *fine* (end), opening or closing repeat signs, etc., have sometimes been supplied to this edition. These additions are enclosed in brackets (e.g., [*Fine*]) or mentioned in the annotations. For the avoidance of doubt, any *fine* marking that appears in the original (which Ole usually indicated with a fermata over a bar line) is indicated here with a *fine* marking. In cases where the "roadmap" remains unclear, it is helpful to remember LeRoy Larson's assertion: "The formal scheme of any performance is not restricted to any one rule of thumb."[4]

OTHER EDITORIAL PRACTICES

Apparent errors in pitch have been altered in the transcriptions and noted in the annotations. Obvious errors in rhythmic value have been silently corrected. Certain modern notational practices were silently applied—for example, pertaining to key signatures and accidentals, and the beaming of notes (connecting several notes with tails via a horizontal line; this applies only to eighth, sixteenth, and thirty-second notes) to render the meter more obvious. Two types of notational abbreviations exist in the original, including *bis* (indicating a short passage should be played twice) and notes with strokes across the stem (indicating they should be subdivided into eighth notes or sixteenth notes). For ease of reading, abbreviations have been silently expanded into full notation. As much as possible, tempo and dynamic indications, slurs, fingerings, articulation marks (at times idiosyncratic), and any other special markings have been reproduced as found in the original.

THE ANNOTATIONS

The annotations include any editorial notes or background information. Brief citations to sources for additional background, notation, or recordings are keyed to full references in the bibliography. Any substantive inscriptions that appear with the tune are described. The annotations also state the page or pages in Ole's manuscript where the tune appears; for example, [OH 10–11] indicates pages 10–11 of the manuscript.

HANDWRITING OF VARIOUS CONTRIBUTORS TO THE MANUSCRIPT

The handwriting of some of the tunes shows that additional musicians, perhaps Ole's children, contributed to the tunebook. Someone with a rounded, possibly feminine hand added eleven tunes, usually in pencil in blank space at the bottom of pages (#25a–b, #29, #47–48, #50, #52, #54, #57, #61, and #68). Someone with an inexperienced hand added #46 and a duplicate of #8c, which appears on page [54]. Someone with a somewhat angular hand added #53, Vals–Lange Stunder. In addition, several statements of attribution have been added to tunes transcribed in Ole's hand; almost all of these later inscriptions are reminiscent of this angular hand. The waltzes on the final four pages of the collection were written by someone with a neat, compact hand (#82 and #83). Three harmony lines on pages [50] and [68], omitted from this edition, appear in yet another hand. All of the remaining 110 tunes (plus ten omitted duplicates, fragments, and harmony lines) appear to be in Ole's own handwriting.

Figure 29. Samples of different handwriting in the tunebook: (a) Ole's hand, [OH 67]; (b) Rounded hand [OH 72]; (c) Inexperienced hand [OH 54]; (d) Angular hand [OH 52]; and (e) Compact hand [OH 97]. Courtesy of Beth Hoven Rotto.

The Transcriptions

1. Quadrille
1a. No. 1

Swen (Sven) Olson

1a. Tunes 1a and 1b appear twice in the manuscript [OH 1, 11]. The notation "By Sven Olson" appears at the bottom of page [1] and seems to apply to both tunes. Swen Olson was Ole's friend, business partner, and frequent musical collaborator in Elbow Lake (see additional information in chap. 1). Recording: New Ole Hendricks Orchestra, *Play It Again, Ole!*, track 1.

1b. No. 2

Swen (Sven) Olson

1b. See note for 1a. An unusual quadrille tune with a change of meter in the last section. Recording: New Ole Hendricks Orchestra, *Play It Again, Ole!*, track 2. [OH 1]

1c. No. 3—Reel [Wake Up Susan]

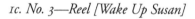

1c. Untitled in the manuscript, this tune is a version of the well-known old-time breakdown Wake Up Susan, which is related to the Irish reel Mason's Apron. Wake Up Susan was played in many parts of the U.S. and appeared in several published collections. At [1], many versions have low A, but Ole has in fact written E. Notation: Ryan, *Ryan's Mammoth Collection* (1883), 45; Christeson, *Old-Time Fiddler's Repertory* (1973), 5; Bayard, *Dance to the Fiddle* (1981), 346–53 (Hell on the Potomac, [1]). For additional background and sources, see Jabbour, *American Fiddle Tunes from the Archive of Folk Song*, 14–15; and Kuntz and Pelliccioni, Traditional Tune Archive, s.v. "Wake Up Susan (1)." [OH 2]

2. [Quadrille:] No. 1

2. This tune apparently was intended for the first figure of a quadrille, but whether Ole used it in a particular set of tunes is unclear. [OH 2]

3. Polka

Attributed to "A. Sornson"

3. The attribution, which does not appear to be in Ole's own handwriting and was probably added later, refers to Anders Sørensen (1821–96). This tune does not appear in the collections of Sørensen's compositions compiled by Gunhildsberg or Sandvik. Nevertheless, it is reminiscent of storgårdsmusikk and likely came from a Norwegian source. Editorial changes: [1] changed from E to F; [2] changed from D to F. The repeat sign at the end of the second part has been supplied to match the repeat sign at the beginning of the second part. The form of this tune is unclear. Presumably,

the first part was reprised to finish the tune, but there are no indications of this in the manuscript. [OH 3]

4. The Grand Set of Quadrilles
4a. No. 1

4a. This tune appears twice in the manuscript [OH 5, 79]. The note at [1] has been changed from C-sharp to B. This tune is preceded by a fragment of a waltz. [OH 5]

4b. No. 2

4b. [OH 5]

4c. No. 3

4c. [OH 6]

5. Quadrille

5a. No. 1

5a. [OH 6]

5b. No. 2

5b. Repeat sign at the beginning has been supplied to match the following repeat sign, although it is not quite clear where the repeat was meant to begin. As shown here, the structure of the tune is ABABCCBA. [OH 7]

5c. No. 3

5c. The repeat signs in the first part have been supplied to balance the repeats in the other sections. [OH 7]

6. Elias [Favorat?] Quadrille
6a. No. 1

6a. [OH 8]

6b. No. 2

6b. This tune was probably played ABACA, although it is unclear whether the sections are to be repeated (manuscript has a single repeat sign, at the very end). [OH 8]

6c. No. 3

6c. [OH 9]

7. Quadrille
7a. No. 1

7a. The B section sounds peculiar but is transcribed here as it appears in the manuscript. [OH 9]

7b. No. 2

7b. [OH 10]

7c. No. 3

Fine

7c. [OH 10–11]

8. Quadrille
8a. No. 1
8a. Tune #1a reappears here as the first tune in this quadrille set. [OH 11]

8b. No. 2
8b. Tune #1b reappears here as the second tune in this quadrille set. [OH 11]

8c. No. 3—Polka

8c. The attribution likely refers to Anders Sørensen; however, this polka does not appear in Sandvik's or Gunhildsberg's collections of Anders Sørensen's compositions. The repeat signs in the third part have been supplied to balance the repeats in the preceding sections. Apparently one of Ole's favorites, this tune appears three times in the manuscript [OH 12, 54, 55]. On page [54], "Pro. Amundsen" seems to be credited as the source of this tune. An additional inscription on page [55] reads, "Jeg." Recording: New Ole Hendricks Orchestra, *Play It Again, Ole!*, track 3.

9. Quadrille
9a. No. 1

9a. [OH 12]

9b. No. 2

[Swen Olson]

9b. This tune appears twice in the manuscript: on page [13], without any attribution, and on page [56], attributed to Swen Olson (see additional information about Olson in chap. 1). Recording: New Ole Hendricks Orchestra, *Play It Again, Ole!*, track 10. [OH 13, 56]

9c. No. 3—Rosendale

9c. Rosendale is the name of towns in New York and in eastern Wisconsin. (Rosendal also happens to be a place in Norway, southeast of Bergen.) Recording: New Ole Hendricks Orchestra, *Play It Again, Ole!*, track 11. [OH 13]

10. Quadrille
10a. No. 1

10a. This tune appears twice in the manuscript [OH 14, 56]. Repeats, *da capo*, and *fine* markings reflect a composite of the two appearances of this tune in the manuscript. Recording: New Ole Hendricks Orchestra, *Play It Again, Ole!,* track 9.

10b. No. 2

10b. There is no indication of whether the A section is to be repeated. Manuscript has unmatched repeat signs at the end of the B section and beginning of C section. Corresponding repeat signs have been supplied at the beginning of the second part and end of the third part. [OH 14]

10c. No. 3

10c. [OH 14–15]

11. Quadrille
11a. No. 1

11a. Manuscript has no repeat signs in the B section. [OH 15]

11b. No. 2

11b. Repeat signs in C part do not appear in the manuscript and have been supplied. [OH 15]

11c. No. 3

11c. The original contains a single repeat sign at the very end. The other repeat signs have been supplied here based on the form of similar tunes in the manuscript. [OH 16]

12. Quadrille
12a. No. 1

12a. [OH 16]

12b. No. 2

12b. The manuscript offers no indication of whether the A section is to be repeated. Repeats in the A section were added based on the form of other tunes in the collection. [OH 17]

12c. No. 3

12c. [OH 17]

13. Quadrille

13a. No. 1

13a. [OH 18]

13b. No. 2

13b. No repeat signs appear in the manuscript. [OH 18]

13c. No. 3

13c. [OH 19]

14. Quadrille
14a. No. 1

14a. No repeat signs appear in the B or C sections of the manuscript. Repeat signs were supplied based on the form of other tunes in the collection. [OH 19]

14b. No. 2

14b. The note at [1] has been changed from A to B. [OH 20]

14c. No. 3

14c. Repeats are clearly marked in the manuscript, but there is no *fine* marking. [OH 20]

15. Quadrille
15a. No. 1

15a. [OH 21]

15b. No. 2

15b. [OH 21]

15c. No. 3

15c. [OH 22]

16. Quadrille
16a. No. 1

16a. [OH 22]

16b. No. 2

16b. [OH 23]

16c. [No. 3]—All Up Reel

16c. [OH 23]

17. Quadrille
17a. No. 1

17a. [OH 24]

17b. No. 2

17b. [OH 24]

17c. No. 3—Sicilian Circle

17c. A Sicilian circle is a dance where pairs of couples form a large circle with the two couples in each pair facing each other. (If the circle were a wheel, each pair of couples would be a spoke in the wheel.) The Sicilian circle was a very social dance, since each couple progressed around the circle, dancing with all of the other couples in succession. The dance, and a number of variations on it, appear in several nineteenth-century American dance manuals (e.g., *Dick's Quadrille Call-book and Ball-Room Prompter*, 113; Rivers, *A Full Description of Modern Dances*, 38). It was frequently danced to a tune in $\frac{6}{8}$ time by the same name (see Howe, *Pianist's Social Circle*, 121; Ford, *Traditional Music of America*, 92). However, other tunes were used for the dance, such as a Gallop for Sicilian Circle, which appeared in Howe's *Musician's Omnibus*, 3:300. Ole's tune is a version of a reel known in the United States and Canada as Levantine's Barrel. See Kuntz and Pelliccioni, *Traditional Tune Archive*, s.v. "Levantine's Barrel," and Bayard, *Dance to the Fiddle*, 206–9 (#247, The Bummer's Reel) for additional background. Notation: Ryan, *Ryan's Mammoth Collection* (1883), 46 (Levantine's Barrel). [OH 25]

18. [Quadrille]

18a. No. 1

18a. No repeats are indicated in the manuscript. [OH 25]

18b. No. 2

18b. *Da capo* marking at the end of the B section has been supplied based on the form of similar three-part tunes in the manuscript. [OH 26]

18c. No. 3

18c. The A section as shown here (especially the first and second endings) is an attempt to reconstruct this tune, which is incomplete in the manuscript. Some of the bar lines in the original were misplaced and have been shifted. [OH 26]

19. [Quadrille]
19a. No. 1—Guildroy

19a. The name of this tune is usually spelled Guilderoy or Gilderoy in other sources. The only tune set in a minor key in the entire manuscript, this reel of Scottish origin became one of the "ironclads" in the repertoire of American fiddlers. Also known as The Red-Haired Boy, it appeared in many manuscripts and published collections. Kuntz and Pelliccioni, Traditional Tune Archive, s.v. "Gilderoy [2]," provide additional background. Notation: Ole's version is very similar to the one in Howe, *Third Part of the Musician's Companion* (1844), 47. Other sources include Howe, *Musician's Omnibus* (1863), 1:43; O'Neill, *O'Neill's Music of Ireland* (1903), 325 (#1748, The Redhaired Boy); Ford, *Traditional Music of America* (1965), 43; Bayard, *Dance to the Fiddle* (1982), 119–22; and several manuscript collections available through the American Vernacular Music Manuscripts, ca. 1730–1910 online archive. [OH 27]

19b. No. 2—Aldridgs Hornpipe [Aldridge's Hornpipe]

19b. Another tune that appeared in many published collections. According to Kuntz and Pelliccioni, the name refers to Robert Aldridge, a stage dancer and dance master active in London and Edinburgh during the eighteenth century (Traditional Tune Archive, s.v. "Aldridge's Hornpipe [1]"). The note at [1] was changed from D to F-sharp. Notation: Ole's version is similar to Howe, *Second Part of the Musician's Companion* (1843), 38. Other sources include Howe, *Musician's Omnibus* (1863), 1:50, and Ryan, *Ryan's Mammoth Collection* (1883), 120. [OH 27]

19c. No. 3

19c. [OH 27]

20. Parish Hornpipe

20. Notation: Howe, *Musician's Omnibus* (1863), 1:53. [OH 28]

21. Vintions Hornpipe [Vinton's Hornpipe]

21. Another hornpipe featured in many published collections, dating back to the eighteenth century. For additional background, see Kuntz, *The Fiddler's Companion*, s.v. "Vinton's Hornpipe." Notation: Howe, *First Part of the Musician's Companion* ([1850]), 61; Howe, *Musician's Omnibus* (1863), 1:45; Ryan, *Ryan's Mammoth Collection* (1883), 124; O'Neill, *O'Neill's Music of Ireland* (1903), 300 (#1618, O'Fenlon's Hornpipe); Ford, *Traditional Music of America* (1965), 109; and Bayard, *Dance to the Fiddle* (1982), 373. [OH 28]

22. College Hornpipe

22. Another standard hornpipe from the Anglo-American fiddle repertoire. Also known as Sailor's Hornpipe, it dates back to the eighteenth century. For additional background, see Kuntz and Pelliccioni, Traditional Tune Archive, s.v. "College Hornpipe." Notation: Howe, *First Part of the Musician's Companion* ([1850]), 49; Howe, *Musician's Omnibus* (1863), 1:45; Ryan, *Ryan's Mammoth Collection* (1883), 120; O'Neill, *O'Neill's Music of Ireland* (1903), 323 (#1737, Jack's the Lad); Ford, *Traditional Music of America* (1965), 46 (Sailor's Hornpipe); and Bayard, *Dance to the Fiddle* (1982), 261–64. [OH 28]

23. [Constitution Hornpipe]

23. This tune bears no title in the manuscript but appears in many American collections as the Constitution Hornpipe. Kuntz (*The Fiddler's Companion,* s.v. "Constitution Hornpipe [1]") suggests that it might have been named for USS *Constitution,* also known as Old Ironsides, the famous frigate of the U.S. Navy launched in 1797 and still afloat. Notation: Howe, *First Part of the Musician's Companion* ([1850]), 58; Howe, *Musician's Omnibus* (1863), 1:45; Ryan, *Ryan's Mammoth Collection* (1883), 153; Ford, *Traditional Music of America* (1965), 95; Christeson, *Old-Time Fiddler's Repertory* (1973), 83; and Bayard, *Dance to the Fiddle* (1982), 75–76 (#138, Reel in F). It appears twice in Ole's manuscript [OH 29, 81].

24. Durange Hornpipe [Durang's Hornpipe]

24. This tune was named for John Durang (1768–1822), the first American dancer of real prominence. Based in Philadelphia, Durang performed in theaters throughout the northeastern United States and also toured Canada. He was immensely popular. His talents extended to acting, acrobatics, and puppetry, but he was best known for dancing the hornpipe.[1] Durang states in his memoirs that Durang's Hornpipe was composed for him by a Mr. Hoffmaster in 1785.[2] Bayard commented that, compared to the original composition, the tune "has been greatly improved by its nearly two centuries' life in tradition. The fiddlers . . . have eliminated the accidentals, reduced the melodic sequences, and made changes that have added considerable musical variety and interest." John Durang's son Charles also made a career in dance and was the author of a number of dance manuals that were published in the 1840s and 1850s.[3] Notation: Howe, *First Part of the Musician's Companion* ([1850]), 59; Howe, *Musician's Omnibus* (1863), 1:43; Ryan, *Ryan's Mammoth Collection* (1883), 128; Ford, *Traditional Music of America* (1965), 53; Christeson, *Old-Time Fiddler's Repertory* (1973), 63; Bayard, *Dance to the Fiddle* (1982), 341–44; and several manuscript collections available through American Vernacular Music Manuscripts, ca. 1730–1910 online archive. [OH 29]

25. Quadrille American Stalwart
25a. No. 2

25a. This tune was added by the unknown contributor with the rounded hand. [OH 29]

25b. No. 4

25b. This tune was added by the unknown contributor with the rounded hand. [OH 30]

26. [Reinlender]

26. The measure at [1] was missing in the original and has been added to match the second half of the A section. There is no *fine* marking in the original. The first twelve bars of this tune, struck through, appear on the same page above Ole's complete transcription. Recording: New Ole Hendricks Orchestra, *Play It Again, Ole!*, track 12. [OH 30]

27. [Polka or Quadrille]

27. No repeats are indicated for this tune. Notes in last measure of the A section were changed from E to D. [OH 31]

28. [Polka or Quadrille]

28. The dotted rhythm at [1] has been supplied to match the dotted rhythm in the following phrase. Repeat signs have been supplied to the first part to match those in the second part. [OH 31]

29. Quadrille Joe Fifer: No. 2

29. This tune was added by the unknown contributor with the rounded hand. [OH 31]

30. Darkes Dream [Darkie's Dream]

30. Darkie's Dream (or Darkey's Dream) is an old-time breakdown or schottische that was played in the southern Appalachians and in Missouri (Kuntz and Pelliccioni, Traditional Tune Archive, s.v. "Darkey's Dream"). This traditional tune is said to have inspired the three-part version composed by the Boston banjo player George Lansing, published as sheet music in various editions beginning in 1889. It is unclear whether Ole might have adapted one of those editions for this setting. The key is the same as in several editions (F major), but Ole's version in ABA form is not a true three-part tune and also lacks any syncopations. George Lansing was the author of several banjo tutors and a partner in L. B. Gatcomb & Co., a Boston firm that made banjos and guitars.[4] Darkie's Dream later resurfaced as a barn dance in the Irish tradition. Notation: Bayard, *Dance to the Fiddle* (1982), 392–94 (#411, The Darkey's Dream). An early edition of Lansing's *The Darkie's Dream* (1891) is available from the Lester S. Levy Sheet Music Collection, where it was cataloged with the very appropriate descriptor "ethnic stereotypes." [OH 32]

31. Whistling Coon

[Sam Devere]

31. Whistling Coon was a song composed by the white vaudeville artist Sam Devere (1842–1907), who had a long career in touring minstrel shows. It was published as sheet music in 1878. Twelve years later, it was recorded on wax cylinder by the first African American recording artist, George W. Johnson (1846–1914). Johnson was discovered by early recording entrepreneurs in 1890 while busking in New York. Tim Brooks, his definitive biographer, relates that Johnson was asked to sing a "'coon song' novelty in which the black man made fun of himself. It is unlikely that Johnson enjoyed singing this insulting song . . . but it always brought a shower of nickels from the white folks. . . . When you were hungry and needed money to eat, you sang whatever they wanted you to."[5] That first song was the jaunty Whistling Coon, which included a refrain that showcased Johnson's talents as a whistler. The Whistling Coon and Johnson's second recording, The Laughing Song, remained best sellers into the mid-1890s. Whether the sheet music or recordings of The Whistling Coon ever reached Ole Hendricks is open to conjecture, but they were distributed nationwide. Since the tune did enter the folk tradition, Ole might have learned it by ear (Kuntz and Pelliccioni, Traditional Tune Archive, s.v. "Whistling Coon"). Notation: Devere, *The Whistling Coon* (ca. 1888). [OH 32]

32. Polka

32. Typical of the polkas in the storgårdsmusikk genre. [OH 33]

33. Polka

Attributed to "H. Balstad"

33. The attribution refers to Hans Balstad (see information about Balstad in chap. 2). Like the preceding tune, this tune is typical of polkas in the storgårdsmusikk genre. The natural sign at [1] has been supplied. Recording: New Ole Hendricks Orchestra, *Play It Again, Ole!*, track 5. [OH 34]

34. Polka

34. Another example of a polka from the storgårdsmusikk genre. The note at [1] was changed from E-sharp to E-natural. [OH 35]

35. Ficher Horn Pipe Copy [Fisher's Hornpipe]

35. One of the most widespread tunes in the Anglo-American fiddle repertory, Fisher's Hornpipe was common in oral tradition and appeared in many
published collections and vernacular manuscripts. According to Alan Jabbour, the tune was composed in England in the eighteenth century by
J. Fishar and published in 1780 (*American Fiddle Tunes from the Archive of
Folk Song*, 8–9). For additional background, see Kuntz and Pelliccioni, *Traditional Tune Archive*, s.v. "Fisher's Hornpipe." Notation: Howe, *First Part
of the Musician's Companion* ([1850]), 50 (in the key of F); Howe, *Musician's
Omnibus* (1863), 1:43 (in F); Ryan, *Ryan's Mammoth Collection* (1883), 130
(in F); Ford, *Traditional Music of America* (1965), 39 (in D); Christeson,
Old Time Fiddler's Repertory (1973), 57 (in D); Bayard, *Dance to the Fiddle*
(1982), 332–34, 573 (multiple settings in D and G); and several manuscript
collections available through American Vernacular Music Manuscripts, ca.
1730–1910 online archive. Recordings: Jabbour, *American Fiddle Tunes from
the Archive of Folk Song*; and Leary, *Folksongs of Another America*. [OH 36]

36. Waltz [Bird Waltz]

Fine

36. This tune, untitled in Ole's manuscript, is named Bird Waltz in Howe's *Musician's Omnibus*. Repeat signs in the second section have been supplied to match the repeats in the first and third sections. Notation: Howe, *Musician's Omnibus* (1863), 1:40 and 2:127. (In Howe's second volume, the tune appears as music for a Spanish-style dance called La Madrilainne.) [OH 36]

37. Reinlender

D.O. Wold

37. A composition by D. O. Wold, who emigrated from Stange in Hedmark to Black River Falls, Wisconsin. Title as originally written is "Reilander By D. O. Vold." See additional information about Wold in chap. 2. Recording: New Ole Hendricks Orchestra, *Play It Again, Ole!*, track 17. [OH 37]

38. Reinlender

Attributed to "A. Sörnsen"

38. The lower note of the double stops at [1] has been changed from F-sharp to A. The attribution, which does not appear to be in Ole's own handwriting and was probably added later, refers to Anders Sørensen. This reinlender, however, does not appear in Sandvik's or Gunhildsberg's collections of Sørensen's works. Thomas Nilssen (personal communication, March 4, 2019) identified it as a variant of a well-known reinlender that was collected by both K. J. Hanssen and Knut Kjøk. Kjøk's source was the fiddler Ola Opheim of Vågå in Gudbrandsdal (Oppland, Norway), and he cited additional connections to Trøndelag. (Kjøk does not associate this tune with Sørensen.) Ole's original transcription might have been made hastily or from an imperfect memory of a performance, since the phrase lengths are irregular and some of the bar lines seem misplaced. To render it playable, the tune as shown here has been conservatively edited based on these two published versions. The editorial changes were primarily metrical; Ole's melody line was simply realigned to fit within the usual reinlender phrase structure. Notation: K. J. Hanssen, *Dans! Ropte Fela!* (1902–7), 5:9 (tune #11); Knut Kjøk, *Slåtte og leikje* (2012), 5:887 (tune #170). [OH 38]

39. Waltz of Spand Berg—Brudens Sorg

Attributed to "A. Sornsen"

39. The attribution, which does not appear to be in Ole's own handwriting and was probably added later, refers to Anders Sørensen. However, this waltz does not appear in Sandvik's or Gunhildsberg's collections of Sørensen's works. Thomas Nilssen (personal communication, March 4, 2019) notes that the style is consistent with Sørensen. This tune is probably associated with Martinus Nielsen Spangberg of Stange (see chap. 2). Additional inscription: "Copy." Recording: New Ole Hendricks Orchestra, *Play It Again, Ole!*, track 8. [OH 39]

40. Waltz

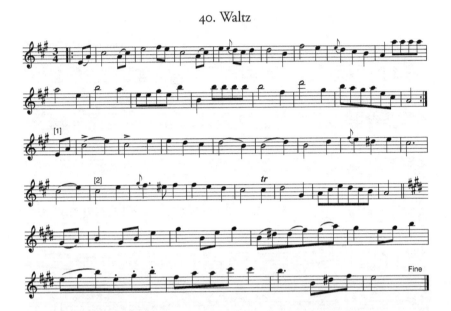

40. At [1], the key signature has been changed from D to A. The measure marked [2] was missing in the manuscript and has been reconstructed based on the previous line. [OH 40]

41. Polka

[From the repertoire of Hans P. Bakstad]

41. This polka is attributed to Hans Balstad in the manuscript; however, it is actually associated with Hans P. Bakstad (1824–1902) of Eidsvoll (see discussion in chap. 2). Notation: Lien Jenssen, *På Budor* (2007), 146: "No. 44, Polket efter Bakstad," taken from the notebook of Hans Borgersen (1862–1947). Recording: New Ole Hendricks Orchestra, *Play It Again, Ole!*, track 19. [OH 41]

42. Waltz

42. Thomas Nilssen (personal communication, March 4, 2019) recognized this tune as an example of a *sekstur*. According to Egil Bakka, a sekstur is a subtype of *engelskdans* (often called *englis*), which had its roots in English dance traditions but became common in Norway at the beginning of the nineteenth century. It would have been a familiar tour dance on large farming estates in Hedmark. The engelskdans is a row dance to a tune in waltz time, usually notated in $\frac{3}{8}$. These compact tunes consist of two, three, or four eight-bar repeated sections, each section corresponding to a figure (or tour) in the dance. One section repeated was equivalent to two figures in the dance. Therefore a three-part tune would suit a six-figure dance, which is a *sekstur* (six tour). Similarly, a two-part tune was called *firetur* (four tour), and a four-part tune an *åttetur* (eight tour). Many of these tunes were later repurposed as waltzes, as in this example.[6] [OH 42]

43. Waltz

A[?]. Nelson

43. This might have been part of an arrangement where other instruments helped carry the melody (some sections here seem more harmonic than melodic in nature). The first and second endings for the second part appear in condensed form in the manuscript. They have been expanded here for greater readability. The note at [1] was changed from low A to C. The last

section is irregular in the manuscript. Additional notation on the manuscript, below the title: "Olmsted." [OH 42–43]

44. Olave Schottische

Attributed to "Sornson"

44. The attribution, which does not appear to be in Ole's own handwriting and was probably added later, refers to Anders Sørensen. However, this tune does not appear in Sandvik's or Gunhildsberg's collections of Sørensen's compositions. Since Sørensen's reinlenders are not typically labeled as schottisches, the attribution seems suspect. In any case, this tune is markedly different in character to Sørensen's known reinlenders. The title, which *is* in Ole's handwriting, is difficult to read in the manuscript. It might be *Olave, Otave,* or even *Octave.* In addition, the notation is imprecise in several places, and the form is unclear. Ole generally used a fermata to indicate a *fine*, but there are two fermatas in this case. I surmise that a *da*

capo was intended after the final bar, and the first three sections were then repeated, with the final cadence on the original tonic note of D. Recording: New Ole Hendricks Orchestra, *Play It Again, Ole!*, track 7. [OH 44]

45. No. 5—Buck and Wing Dance

De Witt

45. The title of this syncopated tune refers to an African American dance that became a staple of minstrel and vaudeville shows of the late nineteenth century. A precursor to modern tap dancing, buck-and-wing dancing included elements from the earlier buck dance, which featured a step that was "very percussive, and weighted down into the foot," and wing dance, in which the dancer's arms and legs moved in a flapping motion.[7] Norton cites additional influences, such as the soft shoe, clog dance, and jig, and states that "any standard 32-bar tune served as a suitable accompaniment."[8] However, this tune is 48 bars in length. Ole's attribution to "De Witt" might refer to the New York sheet music publishers Clinton De Witt or Robert De Witt. The De Witts also published dance manuals, such as Henry Tucker's *Clog Dancing Made Easy* (1874). [OH 45]

46. Rose Lawn

46. This reel or breakdown was added by the unknown contributor with the inexperienced hand. It might have been part of a quadrille set originally. [OH 46]

47. No. 4—Park Avenue

47. This reel or breakdown was added by the unknown contributor with the rounded hand. Like the previous tune, it might have been part of a quadrille set originally. [OH 46]

48. [Quadrille:] No. 1

48. This tune was added by the unknown contributor with the rounded hand. [OH 46]

49. Reinlender

49. This tune was also collected by Edvard Andresen (1849–1929), born in Eidsvoll, Akershus, and later a resident of Tangen in Hedmark. Andresen labeled it "Förste reilender som kom til Norg [*sic*]" (First reinlender that came to Norway) and apparently played it in the lower key of G. Notation: Lien Jenssen, *Gamle notebøker* (1992), 212; Lien Jenssen, *På Budor* (2007), 126. Recording: New Ole Hendricks Orchestra, *Play It Again, Ole!*, track 15. [OH 48]

50. Prairie Queen Quadrille: No. 1

50. This tune was added by the unknown contributor with the rounded hand. The B-sharp at [1] is faintly marked and appears only in the final phrase; it is unclear whether the corresponding note in the previous phrase should also be raised. The Prairie Queen Quadrille was a "fancy" or novelty quadrille danced as early as 1886 in Minnesota.[9] *Dick's Quadrille Call-book and Ball-room Prompter* (1895) states that music for this quadrille could be ordered from S. Brainard's Sons of Chicago, but I have not located any extant copies. [OH 48]

51. Waltz No. 84 (1897)

51. This might have been part of an arrangement where other instruments helped carry the melody (some sections here seem more harmonic than melodic in nature). [OH 49]

52. Waltz—Guelder Roses

52. The guelder rose is the common name for *viburnum opulus*. This tune
was added by the unknown contributor with the rounded hand. This tune
also appears in the same hand on page [47], where it has been struck
through. [OH 51]

53. Vals—Lange Stunder

Attributed to "Sörnsen"

53. This tune was added by the unknown contributor with the angular hand. The attribution refers to Anders Sørensen, but this tune does not appear in Sandvik's or Gunhildsberg's collections of Anders Sørensen's compositions. It is typical of the fancy waltzes in the storgårdsmusikk genre. [OH 52–53]

54. Schottische—Graceful

54. This tune was added by the unknown contributor with the rounded
hand. [OH 53]

55. My Best Girl [Quadrille:] No. 2

55. This quadrille tune did not turn up in my search for printed sources; however, it was recorded by Chet Parker (born 1891 in Grand Rapids, Michigan) on *The Hammer Dulcimer Played by Chet Parker* (1966). In Ole's manuscript, this tune is preceded and followed by reappearances of tune #8c (Quadrille Set: No. 3—Polka). [OH 55]

56. The Ladies' [Favorat?] Quadrille
56a. No. 1

56a. The title of this quadrille set is very difficult to read—perhaps "Ladies' Favorite" was intended. Tune #10a reappears here as the first tune in this set. [OH 56]

56b. No. 2

56b. Tune #9b reappears here as the second tune in this quadrille set. [OH 56]

57. Schottische—True Friendship

57. This tune was added by the unknown contributor with the rounded hand. The manuscript does not indicate the form of this tune. Many schottisches with trios published during this period have a *da capo* at the end and a *fine* just before the trio. Others had a *fine* marking at the end of the trio. [OH 57]

58. Polka

Ole Hendricks

58. This difficult tune, the only known composition of Ole Hendricks, is probably a good indication of his technical ability. Recording: New Ole Hendricks Orchestra, *Play It Again, Ole!*, track 16. [OH 58]

59. Waltz—Björneblaken

[Lars Hollo]

59. This vals, unattributed in the manuscript, is a composition of Lars Hollo (see additional information in chap. 2). "Björneblaken" is penciled in, probably by someone other than Ole. The flat sign at [1] was supplied after comparison to other sources. The placement of the *fine* is based on the version reproduced in Lien Jenssen. Faukstad's recording, however, concludes at the end of the first part, and Odde and Nilssen conclude at the end of the third part (although both recordings are based on the version in the notebook of Torger Olstad [1864–1941] of Sel, Gudbrandsdalen). Notation: Lien Jenssen, *Gamle notebøker* (1992), 165 (titled "Björn Blakken vals L. Hollo"); Sandvik, "Lars Hollo: Danser" (titled "Björneblak Vals"); and "12 Danser af L. Holo" (1872) (titled simply, "Vals"). Recordings: Jon Faukstad and Per Sæmund Bjørkum, *Slåtter frå Torger Olstads notebok*, track 14 (Bjørneblakken); Bjørn Kåre Odde and Ole Nilssen, *Hand,* track 2 (Bjørn

Blakkens vals); and New Ole Hendricks Orchestra, *Play It Again, Ole!*, track 18. [OH 59]

60. Waltz

Attributed to "Sörnsen"

60. The attribution, which does not appear to be in Ole's own handwriting and was probably added later, refers to Anders Sørensen. However, this waltz

does not appear in Sandvik's or Gunhildsberg's collections of Sørensen's works. Nevertheless, it is typical of waltzes in the storgårdsmusikk genre and probably came from a Norwegian source. Additional inscriptions in the upper right: "Oldberg" and "Copy." Inscription following the final bar: "Elbow Lake 1891." "Oldberg" might refer to a member of the Olberg family. Kristian Olberg (born 1787) was an important figure in the early development of ensemble music in the area around Lake Mjøsa. He was a precursor to Sørensen and Lars Hollo (Feiring and Feiring, *Fra menuett til masurka*, 85). [OH 60–61]

61. Waltz—Star of Bethlehem

61. This tune was added by the unknown contributor with the rounded hand. The two high A's at [1] were changed from B-flat. This waltz is preceded in the manuscript by what appears to be a harmony for an unidentified waltz and another, incomplete waltz. [OH 62–63]

62. Waltz

[Martinus Nielsen Spangberg?]

62. This vals is attributed to "M. Spangberg" in the manuscript and might have been associated with Martinus Nielsen Spangberg of Stange (see additional information about Spangberg in chap. 2). The note at [1] is illegible on the manuscript; it might have been a high B or high D. This tune is a bit unusual and may have been a part of an arrangement where the melody was carried by various instruments in turn. The triple stops at [2] are quite peculiar. Despite its unusual nature, this piece is evidence that Ole's tunebook includes material sourced from Martinus Spangberg and is thus another link to Hedmark in Norway. [OH 64]

63. Vals

Attributed to "Balstad"

63. I have been unable to verify the attribution of this tune to Hans Balstad; however, it is typical of waltzes in the storgårdsmusikk genre. An additional notation in the manuscript, "Spenberg #4," might indicate an association with Martinus Nielsen Spangberg of Stange (see additional information about Spangberg in chap. 2). Recording: New Ole Hendricks Orchestra, *Play It Again, Ole!*, track 6. [OH 64–65]

64. Reinlender

64. The note at [1] was changed from D to C. Additional inscription to the right of the title: "Copy." Thomas Nilssen identified this tune as one recorded by Jon Faukstad, whose source was Iver Krukhaug (1909–95) of Heidal in Gudbrandsdalen in Norway. Iver learned the tune from his father, who got it from one of the great fiddlers from the same area, Hans Sletmo (1825–94). Faukstad's version starts on what is Ole's second part. Recording: Jon Faukstad (with Per Sæmund Bjørkum, fiddle), *Norske drag: Folkemusikk på akkordeon*, track 14. [OH 65]

65. Vals

Attributed to "A. Sörnsen"

65. Another vals from the storgårdsmusikk genre. The attribution, which does not appear to be in Ole's own handwriting and was probably added later, refers to Anders Sørensen. However, this tune does not appear in Sandvik's or Gunhildsberg's collections of Anders Sørensen's compositions. [OH 66]

66. Polka

D.O. Wold

66. A polka by D. O. Wold, who emigrated from Stange in Hedmark to Black River Falls, Wisconsin (see additional information about Wold in chap. 2). Additional inscription in the manuscript after the final bar: "Elbow Lake Minnesota." This tune is followed in the manuscript by three fragments on pages [68–69], written in other hands, that have been omitted from this edition. Recording: New Ole Hendricks Orchestra, *Play It Again, Ole!*, track 13. [OH 67]

67. [Waltz]

67. This extravagant waltz incorporates the Anglo-American fiddle tune
Arkansas Traveler (see section in D-flat). [OH 70–71]

68. Waltz–Mary's Best Fellow

68. This tune was added by the unknown contributor with the rounded hand. The following editorial changes were made: [1] changed from A-natural to B-natural; [2] the E was added to reconstruct this incomplete measure; [3] changed from D to E-flat; [4] changed from C to D; and the sharp sign at [5] was supplied. [OH 72]

69. Ida Schottische

69. Manuscript contains no *fine* marking for this tune. Additional inscription: "Copy." [OH 73]

70. Schottische Crescent

70. Manuscript has no *da capo* or *fine* markings. Last section in C major could be considered a trio and *fine* placed just before it. The dotted rhythm at [1] was supplied (these two beats are eighth notes in the manuscript). The title as originally written is "Schottisch Cresent." This tune was known elsewhere in the Upper Midwest: it also appears in the Johan Arndt (Mostad) (1833–1909) manuscript in the collection of Beth Hoven Rotto. Arndt settled in Winneshiek County, Iowa. Arndt's version includes an additional section, apparently a coda. Recording: New Ole Hendricks Orchestra, *Play It Again, Ole!*, track 4. [OH 74]

71. Bergens Vals [Hilsen til Födehjemmet]

Anders Sørensen

71. Attributed to "A. Sörnson," this is indeed a composition of Anders Sørensen, whose original title was Hilsen til Födehjemmet. Sandvik's 1927 edition of Sørensen compositions, which includes this tune and was published during Ole's lifetime, does not appear to be the source for Ole's version of this tune. After comparison to other sources, the note at [1] was changed from B to C-sharp (see additional information about Sørensen in chap. 2). Notation: Sandvik, *Anders Sørensens danser* (1927) (#3, Hilsen til Barndomshjemmet); Gunhildsberg, *Anders Sørensen's danser* (1984), 17; Anders Haugen, "Manuskripten: Danse af Anders Sörensen for fiolin" (#3, Hilsen til Födehjemmet); Jo[h]n Stulen, "Dansemusikk for fiolin (og bass)," [42] and [80]; and Feiring and Feiring, *Fra menuett til masurka* (1991), N254 (#398, Hilsen til födehjemmet). Recordings: Anders Grøthes Ensemble, *Danser i gammel stil av Anders Sørensen og Ole Rønning*, track 3; New Ole Hendricks Orchestra, *Play It Again, Ole!*, track 14. [OH 75]

72. Fandango of Bergirsen

[Anders Sørensen?]

72. According to Gunhildsberg, this is a composition of Anders Sørensen. Ole attributed it to "Bergirsen," and the name Bergerson is cited in two other sources: O. M. Sandvik's personal copy of his own edition of Sørensen tunes (National Library of Norway, Mus.ms.a 2717), which contains numerous corrections and additions, including a penciled attribution to "Bergersen"; and Anders Haugen's manuscript, also at the National Library of Norway, which states that this tune is "af Bergersen & Sörensen." Perhaps both were involved—Bergerson may have composed it, while Sørensen adapted or arranged it. Although Sandvik's edition was published in 1927 during Ole's lifetime, it does not appear to be the source for Ole's version of this tune. The fandango was a type of *turdanser* (see information about *turdanser* and about Sørensen in chap. 2). Notation: Anders Haugen, "Manuskripten"; Sandvik, *Anders Sørensens danser* (1927), #18; Gunhildsberg, *Anders Sørensen's danser* (1984), 23. [OH 76]

73. Figaro of C. Brogger

[Niels Christian Brøgger]

73. A composition of Niels Christian Brøgger (1783–1827), a waldhorn player who worked in Christiania and Christianssand. He is said to have composed a variety of dance music, but none of it was ever published. This figaro, however, survived in the oral tradition.[10] The figaro was a type of *turdanser*. (The turdanser genre and Brøgger are discussed in chap. 2.) The second measure is incomplete in Ole's manuscript and has been reconstructed. Repeats for the first two sections have been supplied. Notation: Semb, *Norske folkedansar: Turdansar* (1991), 209 and 384 (in C); Lien Jenssen, *Gamle notebøker* (1992), 53 (in A), 146 (in C), and 191 (in C). Recordings: *Norske Turdansar: Kontradansar frå Austlandet; By- og Storgårdsmusikk*

frå 1800-talet, track 10; New Ole Hendricks Orchestra, *Play It Again, Ole!*, track 20. [OH 77]

74. Klingenberg Polka

74. The opening repeat sign in the last section has been supplied. Feiring and Feiring associate this tune with musicians from Brøttum in Ringsaker, Hedmark (approximately eight miles south of Lillehammer). They include this tune in a section of repertoire from Nils T. Midtlien (1875–1943), a noted tradition bearer from nearby Lismarka who transcribed a number of

dance tunes from the nineteenth century and wrote about older musicians from the area.[11] Incidentally, this tune is unrelated to two works with similar titles by Norwegian composers: the Klingenberg Polka-Mazurka of Rikard Nordraak (1842–66) and the Klingenberg Salon-Polka of Johan Svendsen (1840–1911). In Ole's manuscript, this tune is followed by a repeat of tune #4a (The Grand Set of Quadrilles: No. 1). Notation: Feiring and Feiring, *Fra menuett til masurka* (1991), N159 (#247, Klingenbergs Polket); Jevnager, "Dansemusikk for fiolin," 129 (#238, Klingenbergs Salon Polka). [OH 78–79]

75. Quadrille
75a. No. 1

75a. The note at [1] was changed from E-flat to E-natural. No repeat signs appear in the manuscript for this tune. [OH 80]

75b. No. 2

75b. The note at [1] was changed from E-sharp to E-natural. [OH 81]

75c. No. 3

75c. Tune #23, [Constitution Hornpipe], reappears here as the third tune in this quadrille set. [OH 81]

76. Oriental Quadrille
76a. No. 1

76a. [OH 82]

76b. No. 2

76b. No repeats are indicated in manuscript. [OH 82]

76c. No. 3

76c. No repeats are indicated in the B or C sections. [OH 83]

76d. No. 4

76d. No repeats are marked in the original. [OH 83]

77. Quadrille
77a. No. 1

77a. No repeats are indicated in the manuscript. [OH 84]

77b. No. 2

77b. No repeats are indicated in the manuscript. The note at [1] was changed from C-sharp to D. [OH 84–85]

77c. No. 3

77c. [OH 85]

78. Quadrille: No. 1

78. Only one repeat sign appears in the original; where the repeated section was actually meant to begin is unclear. The tune for the second figure that followed this tune is incomplete and has been omitted. [OH 86]

79. 6th Lancers—Annette
79a. No. 1

[H. Emmel; E.C. Walston, arr.]

79a. The Lancers is a variant of the quadrille. The melody in #79a–d matches the first violin part in a performing edition of *6th Lancers—Annette* published by J. W. Pepper. This edition also included music for a fifth figure that Ole did not transcribe. Little is known about H. Emmel, other than he composed several marches, a polka, and a quick step for band between 1882 and 1903. Ernest C. Walston also composed a handful of works for band but seems to have been more active as an arranger.[12] Several of his arrangements for various instrumental combinations were published during the 1870s and 1880s. He appears in the Philadelphia city directory for 1879. No repeats appear in Ole's or the published versions. Notation: Emmel, *6th Lancers—Annette* (1882). [OH 87]

79b. No. 2

[H. Emmel; E.C. Walston, arr.]

79b. See note for 79a. [OH 87]

79c. No. 3

[H. Emmel; E.C. Walston, arr.]

79c. See note for 79a. [OH 88]

79d. No. 4

[H. Emmel; E.C. Walston, arr.]

79d. See note for 79a. The first measure was condensed from other parts in the arrangement. This tune is followed in the manuscript by a fragment of a waltz that has been omitted from this edition. [OH 88]

80. Life Is a Dream Waltz

[Friedrich Zikoff]

80. Friedrich Zikoff (1824–77) came from Thorn, West Prussia (now Toruń in northern Poland). He had a long career as a leader of military bands and composer of band music.[13] Often in dance genres such as gallop, quadrille, or mazurka, his compositions were familiar to musicians in Norway, to judge by their inclusion in a number of nineteenth-century fiddlers' notebooks. For example, the notebook compiled by Severin Jevnager of Elverum, Hedmark contains a reinlender, polka, waltz, and two gallops by Zikoff.[14] His compositions were also available as sheet music from various publishers in the United States. Notation: Zikoff, *Life Is a Dream* (1879) (a shorter version for parlor organ); Zikoff, *Life Is a Dream* (ca.1876–1887) (a version for piano). [OH 90–92]

81. Andanto [&?] Schottische

81. Judging from the existence of published sheet music for various andante and schottische arrangements, "Andanto" may have referred to the first section, which might have been marked "Andante" or "Andantino." Editorial changes: [1] changed from D-sharp to C-sharp; [2] changed from C-natural to C-sharp, based on the same figure, an octave lower, in mm. 1 and 5. [OH 93–94]

82. [Waltzes]

82. This set of waltzes was added by the unknown contributor with the compact hand. Sets of waltzes like this one appeared in published collections (for example, the section of "Full Sets of Waltzes" in Howe, *The Pianist's Social Circle*, 63–91). The note at [1] was changed from B-sharp to B-natural. [OH 94–96]

83. Vals of Sörnsen [Den ubemærkte]

Anders Sørensen

83. Although incomplete in the manuscript, this is indeed a composition of Anders Sørensen, who also called it Min Første vals (My First Waltz). It became widely known as Sørensen's Waltz. Sandvik's 1927 edition of Sørensen compositions, which includes this tune and was published during Ole's lifetime, does not appear to be the source for the version of this tune in his manuscript. The fourth section, with its plethora of trills, is unusual when compared to other versions. This tune was added to Ole's notebook by the unknown contributor with the compact hand. The manuscript stops just before [4] in the fifth section; the rest of the melody (from [4] to the end) has been reconstructed based on Sørensen's autograph score as reproduced by Gunhildsberg. The anacruses at [2] were supplied based on the autograph. After comparison to all other sources, the top note of the double stop at [1] was changed from C-sharp to D, and the note at [3] was changed from D to C-sharp. The note at [5] is high C-sharp in several other sources, but Sørensen's D is retained here (see additional information about Anders Sørensen in chap. 2). LeRoy Larson collected two settings of this tune in Minnesota, where a less violinistic version entered oral tradition. Notation: Sandvik, *Anders Sørensens danser* (1927), #1; Gunhildsberg, *Anders Sørensens danser* (1984), 8; "Dansemusikk; Fiolinmusikk," 32; Anders Haugen, "Manuskripten" (#1, Den ubemærkte); Feiring and Feiring, *Fra menuett til masurka* (1991), N4 (#6, Vals, Den ubenevnte); and Larson, "Scandinavian-American Folk Dance Music" (1975), 252–53 (#64) and 389–91 (#155, Ole Moe's Waltz). Recordings: Birger Lundbys Ensemble, *Hedemarksmusikk*, track 6; Kåre Korneliussen and Harry Borgen, *Trekkspillvirtuosene Kåre Korneliussen og Harry Borgen*, track 12; Bjørn Kåre Odde and Ole Nilssen, *Hand*, track 5. [OH 97]

Notes

INTRODUCTION

1. This accident actually occurred in the spring of the year, as related in "Town and Country News," *Grant County Herald*, March 9, 1893.

2. "Walcott," *Richland County Gazette*, December 28, 1888.

3. Foot-Notes, *My Father Was a Fiddler*, released 1998, compact disc.

4. Beth Hoven Rotto, personal communication, October 24, 2016.

5. William Henley, *Universal Dictionary of Violin and Bow Makers* (Brighton, UK: Amati Publishing, 1973), 996; Karel Jalovec, *Encyclopedia of Violin-Makers* (London: Paul Hamlyn, 1968), 2:212.

6. Beth Hoven Rotto, personal communication, April 24, 2016.

7. Ole's fiddle is similar to another example at the National Museum of American History, identified as coming from Markneukirchen. See "Russian Model Violin," National Museum of American History website.

8. Paul Dahlin, personal communication, July 2, 2018.

9. Rotto, personal communication, October 24, 2016.

10. "Death Comes to A. O. Svien at 83," *Fergus Falls Daily Journal*, April 20, 1965. Andrew (baptized Anders) Oveson Svien was born in Dennison, Minnesota. His obituary, as well as other records documenting the Svien family's origins in Vang, are available on Ancestry.com.

11. *Standard Atlas of Grant County, Minnesota* (Chicago: Geo. A. Ogle, 1900).

12. Orvin Svien, "The Fiddle," unpublished manuscript, no date, in the possession of Beth Hoven Rotto. Orv recalled hearing the two play for a dance at Prohoskey's Resort on Ten Mile Lake, about ten miles north of Elbow Lake. When he learned this project was in progress, Orv excitedly reminisced, "I could almost see the rosin dust fall from the Heavens as my Uncle Andrew would get his bow in shape to play second fiddle to Ole" (Orvin Svien, personal communication to Beth Hoven Rotto, June 11, 2014).

13. Rotto, personal communication, October 24, 2016.

14. As told by Quentin Hendricks to his daughter Tammy in May 2014 (Tammy Hendricks Creasy, personal communication, May 19, 2014).

15. This letter and a receipt for the purchase are in the possession of Beth Hoven Rotto.

16. Svien, "The Fiddle."

17. Rotto, personal communication, October 24, 2016.

FROM NORWAY TO A LITTLE DANCE HALL ON THE PRAIRIE

1. This information is based on: Baptismal record for Ole, son of Andreas Henriksen and Helge Olsdatter, Sauherad Parish, Telemark, Norway, March 9, 1851; Birger Kirkeby, *Bygdebok for Sauherad: Gards- og Ættesoge* (Sauherad, Norway: Sauherad Kommune, 1980–88), 3:130; and U.S. federal census records for 1870 and 1880. Not unusually, Andreas's name can be found spelled in various ways: Henriksson, Hendricksen, Hendrickson, etc. Andreas was the first child of Henrik Andresson (from Holla in Telemark, ca. 1792–1872) and Tale Tallaksdatter (ca. 1792–1836). I am indebted to Jim Hove for first locating the relevant records in the Digitalarkivet and sharing his genealogical expertise.

2. Odd S. Lovoll, *Across the Deep Blue Sea: The Saga of Early Norwegian Immigrants* (St. Paul: Minnesota Historical Society Press, 2015), 55.

3. Carlton C. Qualey and Jon A. Gjerde, "The Norwegians," in *They Chose Minnesota: A Survey of the State's Ethnic Groups*, ed. June Drenning Holmquist (St. Paul: Minnesota Historical Society Press, 1981), 220–21; B. Lindsay Lowell, "The Scandinavians," in *Encyclopedia of American Social History*, ed. Mary Kupiec Cayton, Elliott J. Gorn, and Peter W. Williams (New York: Charles Scribner's Sons, 1993), 2:703.

4. The family left Sauherad on May 30, 1854, according to the *utflyttede* (out migration) record in the Sauherad Ministerialbok nr. I 7, 1851–73, p. 254, accessed from the Digitalarkivet service of the National Archives of Norway.

5. Lovoll, *Across the Deep Blue Sea*, 47, 83–84, 86, 100–102.

6. Richard J. Fapso, *Norwegians in Wisconsin*, rev. ed. (Madison: Wisconsin Historical Society Press, 2001), 10–13; and Ann Marie Legreid, "Community Building, Conflict, and Change: Geographic Perspectives on the Norwegian-American Experience in Frontier Wisconsin," in *Wisconsin Land and Life*, ed. Robert C. Ostergren and Thomas R. Vale (Madison: University of Wisconsin Press, 1997), 305.

7. The first church was the Portland Norwegian Lutheran Church. Portland Lutheran Church is now located on the site, and Andreas and Helga Hendriksen are buried in the cemetery there. For the early history of Portland, see Monroe County Bicentennial Committee, *Monroe County, Wisconsin, Pictorial History, 1976* (Tomah, WI: Tomah Journal, 1976), 111–16; and Randolph A. Richards, ed.,

History of Monroe County, Wisconsin: Past and Present, Including an Account of the Cities, Towns and Villages of the County (Chicago: C. F. Cooper, 1912; Evansville, IN: Unigraphic, 1977), 529–30, 580.

8. Fapso, *Norwegians in Wisconsin*, 15; and *Map of the La Crosse and Milwaukee Rail Road and Connections* (New York: J. H. Colton, 1855), Library of Congress Geography and Map Division.

9. Philip Martin, *Farmhouse Fiddlers: Music and Dance Traditions in the Rural Midwest* (Mount Horeb, WI: Midwest Traditions, 1994), 118–21.

10. These later years of Ole Bull's life are chronicled by Einar Haugen and Camilla Cai in *Ole Bull: Norway's Romantic Musician and Cosmopolitan Patriot* (Madison: University of Wisconsin Press, 1993), 166–97. Coverage of Ole Bull's appearances in early newspapers is easily retrieved through services such as Chronicling America and the Minnesota Digital Newspaper Hub. Incidentally, Ole Bull's son, Alexander Bull, would eventually appear in concert in Elbow Lake, reportedly playing his father's favorite instrument ("Town and Country News," *Grant County Herald*, March 5, 1896).

11. Øystein Gaukstad and Bjørn Aksdal, "Myllarguten," in *Store norske leksikon*, last updated December 11, 2019; Magne Myhren, "Lars Fykerud," in *Store norske leksikon*, last updated February 13, 2009.

12. Maps showing the historical "territories" of the two instruments can be found in Chris Goertzen, *Fiddling for Norway: Revival and Identity* (Chicago: University of Chicago Press, 1997), xii, and in the endpapers for Olav Sæta, ed., *Norwegian Folk Music, Series II: Slåtter for the Normal Fiddle*, vol. 4, *Hedmark* (Oslo: Universitetsforlaget, 1997). The Hardanger fiddle is primarily played in southern Norway, north and west of Oslo. The regular fiddle is played everywhere else, with a small area of overlap along the west coast, where both instruments are played. More recently, as noted by Vollsnes, these distinctions have become less pronounced as technology and mass media have contributed to the exchange of music across these boundaries. See Arvid O. Vollsnes, "Norway—Music and Musical Life," in *Norway: Society and Culture*, 2nd ed., ed. Eva Maagerø and Birte Simonsen (Kristiansand: Portal, 2008), 285.

13. Howard Wight Marshall, *Play Me Something Quick and Devilish: Old-Time Fiddlers in Missouri* (Columbia: University of Missouri Press, 2012), 263–64; Victor Greene, *A Passion for Polka: Old-Time Ethnic Music in America* (Berkeley: University of California Press, 1992), 21–22.

14. Marshall, *Play Me Something Quick and Devilish*, 254. Singing schools as an important early form of music education are explored in Patricia Jo Kinman Avery, "An Investigation of Music Education Rudiments in Selected American Tunebooks of the Eighteenth and Nineteenth Century: 1700 to 1900" (DMA diss., Shenandoah University, 2001).

15. Monroe County Marriage Records Index (1854–1968), accessed November 2, 2018, Monroe County Local History Room and Museum. Elizabeth's family were among the first settlers to Portland. Her father, Erick Peterson, was a colorful figure, prominent in the community, and is profiled in Richards, *History of Monroe County, Wisconsin* (1912), 834–35.

16. The family appears in the 1885 Dakota Territorial Census, Walcott, Richland County, digital image accessed from North Dakota, Territorial and State Censuses, 1885, 1915, 1925 database on Ancestry.com, s.v. "Henrikson, Ole." Their then-youngest child Henry had been born in Dakota one year earlier. The original town site was surveyed in November 1880, according to Margareth Olson Lahren in *A History of Walcott, North Dakota* ([Wahpeton, ND]: Richland County Historical Society, 1975), 1. Despite his name appearing as Henrikson in the territorial census, Ole was generally known as Ole Hendricks by this time.

17. Caroline Fraser, *Prairie Fires: The American Dreams of Laura Ingalls Wilder* (New York: Metropolitan Books, 2017), 93–94.

18. Gilbert C. Fite, *The Farmers' Frontier, 1865–1900* (New York: Holt, Rinehart and Winston, 1966), 96.

19. Kenneth M. Hammer, "Come to God's Country: Promotional Efforts in Dakota Territory, 1861–1889," *South Dakota History* 10, no. 4 (Fall 1980): 295–302.

20. Ole's and Halvor's families apparently shared a house for at least part of their time in Walcott. An 1885 news item states that "Hendricks Bros. have just completed the decoration of their house" ("Walcott," *Richland County Gazette*, June 26, 1885).

21. Fite, *Farmers' Frontier*, 98. It is unclear whether Ole ever applied for land under the Homestead Act of 1862; however, a search of the records of the Bureau of Land Management's General Land Office at https://glorecords.blm.gov/ indicates that he never proved up on a claim.

22. Duane R. Lindberg, "Pastors, Prohibition and Politics: The Role of Norwegian Clergy in the North Dakota Abstinence Movement, 1880–1920," *North Dakota Quarterly* 49 (Autumn 1981): 32.

23. See the "Walcott" column in the *Richland County Gazette* for December 28, 1888; January 4, 1889; and March 22, 1889.

24. In the 1885 territorial census, the Steelhammers appear only two households away from Ole. Andrew Steelhammer is well documented in subsequent federal censuses and other records available on Ancestry.com, which show that he eventually relocated to Marion County, Oregon.

25. "Walcott and Barrie," *Richland County Gazette*, March 6, 1885; and "Walcott," *Richland County Gazette*, September 18, 1885.

26. The local newspapers mention Ole Hendricks and Andrew Steelhammer traveling together to Wahpeton or Fargo on various occasions. See "From Walcott,"

Wahpeton Times, July 28, 1887, and "Walcott," *Richland County Gazette*, January 4, 1889.

27. Martin, *Farmhouse Fiddlers*, 39.

28. "County Commissioners' Proceedings," *Wahpeton Times*, June 6, 1884.

29. "Walcott Items," *Richland County Gazette*, March 18, 1887.

30. "A Grand Result," *Richland County Gazette*, November 11, 1887.

31. "County Commissioners," *Richland County Gazette*, January 18, 1889; and "County DADS," *Wahpeton Times*, January 10, 1889.

32. "Walcott," *Richland County Gazette*, February 8, 1889.

33. "From Walcott," *Wahpeton Times*, June 23, 1887.

34. "Walcott Items," *Richland County Gazette*, March 18, 1887; "Town and County News," *Grant County Herald*, January 29, 1891.

35. Qualey and Gjerde, "The Norwegians," 226, 228; *Illustrated Souvenir of Grant County* (Elbow Lake: Grant County Herald, 1896), 5.

36. See Fite, *Farmers' Frontier*, 108, and the "Walcott" column in the *Richland County Gazette* for August 26 and September 9, 1887. According to Fraser, "By 1889, the Great Dakota Boom had imploded," mainly due to the arid climate (*Prairie Fires*, 153).

37. "Walcott Items," *Richland County Gazette*, March 18, 1887.

38. "From Walcott," *Wahpeton Times*, June 23, 1887.

39. "Town and County News," *Grant County Herald*, November 20, 1890.

40. "Town and County News," *Grant County Herald*, November 13, 1890.

41. *Illustrated Souvenir of Grant County*, 26; and Bill Goetzinger, *Elbow Lake: The First 100 Years, 1887–1987* (Elbow Lake, MN: Elbow Lake Centennial Committee, 1987), 23.

42. Farm machinery, like agriculture itself, was no doubt a challenging line of business. The following announcement placed by Ole in the November 10, 1892, issue of the *Grant County Herald* suggests that some of their customers were undercapitalized and thus might be a clue as to why this partnership does not seem to have lasted beyond a couple of years: "Lost.—On Tuesday, November 1st, two notes. One a Piano Machine note, given for two binders, payable to me and signed by Geo. P. Jacobs, for $240. The other is a Deering Machine note in payment for a mower, given by Erick Engebretson, for $45. All parties are given notice not to purchase or honor said notes."

43. The average cost for a liquor license in Minnesota was much higher due to the High License Law of 1887, which required those who sold liquor in cities with a population of 10,000 or more to pay $1,000 annually. Elbow Lake's population was under this threshold; nevertheless, Ole paid this amount—twice what he had paid in Walcott—in 1893 and again in 1894. See the "Town and County News" columns in the *Grant County Herald*, April 6, 1893; April 16, 1894; and April 4,

1895. The politics behind the High License Law are discussed in Sabine N. Meyer, *We Are What We Drink: The Temperance Battle in Minnesota* (Urbana: University of Illinois Press, 2015), 59–62. The law was, of course, a legal and financial hurdle to running a saloon. Those who opposed it maintained that it discriminated against immigrants and the laboring class.

44. "Town and County News," *Grant County Herald*, November 27, 1890.

45. Like his brother, Halvor was musical, playing the baritone and perhaps other instruments. Ole Thompson played the cornet, was a part-time band director in the area and also worked in the building trades. He and Ole Hendricks might have played music together in Walcott, since a carpenter named Ole Thompson appears among Ole Hendricks's neighbors in the 1885 Dakota territorial census. Jack McQuillan played the tuba and was involved in local theatrical events. Thompson and McQuillan were likely proficient on other instruments. See Goetzinger, *Elbow Lake*, 73, and "Town and County News" column in the *Grant County Herald* for December 15, 1892; March 7, 1895; and April 9, 1896; and "Hick'ry Farm," *Grant County Herald*, February 11, 1892.

46. "Town and County News," *Grant County Herald*, January 1, 1891.

47. "Town and County News," *Grant County Herald*, January 15, 1891.

48. Bob Skiba, "Here, Everybody Dances: Social Dancing in Early Minnesota," *Minnesota History* 55 (Spring 1997): 220–21.

49. "The Business Men's Banquet," *Grant County Herald*, March 2, 1893.

50. Phil Jamison, *Hoedowns, Reels, and Frolics: Roots and Branches of Southern Appalachian Dance* (Champaign: University of Illinois Press, 2015), 118–19.

51. "The Masquerade," *Grant County Herald*, March 15, 1894.

52. "Fourth of July," *Grant County Herald*, July 11, 1895.

53. LeRoy Wilbur Larson, "Scandinavian-American Folk Dance Music of the Norwegians in Minnesota" (PhD diss., University of Minnesota, 1975), 7–15; Martin, *Farmhouse Fiddlers*, 24–25.

54. "Things as They Occur: Melange of Facts and Fancies, Thoughts and Local Events," *Grant County Herald*, January 18, 1900.

A Trove of Tunes

1. Chris Goertzen, *George P. Knauff's Virginia Reels and the History of American Fiddling* (Jackson: University Press of Mississippi, 2017), 38.

2. Orvin Svien, personal communication to Beth Hoven Rotto, October 6, 2013. The check Andrew Svien wrote for the purchase of Ole's fiddle (see fig. 2) provides a convenient writing sample. The tunebook does not contain any writing that resembles Andrew's.

3. Goertzen, *Knauff's Virginia Reels*, 42.

4. Marshall, *Play Me Something Quick and Devilish*, 65.

5. Anna C. Rue, "From Revival to Remix: Norwegian American Folk Music and Song" (PhD diss., University of Wisconsin–Madison, 2014), 104–5.

6. Alix Cordray, "Survey of Norwegian Dance"; and "Dance Forms," Hardanger Fiddle Association of America.

7. Philip Nusbaum, "Norwegian Traditional Music in Minnesota," in *American Musical Traditions*, ed. Jeff Todd Titon and Bob Carlin (New York: Schirmer Reference, 2002), 4:113; Philip Martin, "Hoppwaltzes and Homebrew: Traditional Norwegian American Music from Wisconsin," in *Wisconsin Folklore*, ed. James P. Leary (Madison: University of Wisconsin Press, 1998), 263. At least four Hardanger fiddle players gave concerts in Elbow Lake during Ole's time: Halvor Solum in 1894 ("Town and County News," *Grant County Herald*, February 22, 1894), Kittel Lear in 1899 ("Things as They Occur," *Grant County Herald*, January 19, 1899), Eivind Aakhus (news item, *Grant County Herald*, January 10, 1907), and Olav Moe (advertisement, *Grant County Herald*, March 7, 1907). These concerts were not always well attended; Leer was billed as an "able interpreter of ancient and classic Norse music," but a follow-up performance in 1900 was canceled because there was not enough of an audience present (see "Things as They Occur," January 11 and January 18, 1900).

8. Martin Ulvestad, *Norge i Amerika med kart: Oplysninger om de norske Amerikanere* (Minneapolis: Norge i Amerika Publishing, 1901), 175.

9. Odd S. Lovoll, *Norwegians on the Prairie: Ethnicity and the Development of the Country Town* (St. Paul: Minnesota Historical Society Press in cooperation with the Norwegian-American Historical Association, 2006), 65.

10. Martin, *Farmhouse Fiddlers*, 47.

11. Goertzen, *Fiddling for Norway*, 106.

12. Arild Hoksnes, *Vals til tusen: Gammaldansmusikken gjennom 200 år* (Oslo: Norske Samlaget, 1988), 23–27; Sæta, *Norwegian Folk Music*, 4:68–69; and Olav Sæta, "Fra halling til reinlender: Historisk skisse av runddansens / gammaldansens inntog i norske danse- og instrumentaltradisjoner" (unpublished manuscript, last updated November 24, 2010), 3. Grundset Fair, near Elverum in Hedmark, was one of the largest country markets. Held annually in March, it attracted people from all over Norway who came to buy and sell horses, timber, textiles, and many other commodities.

13. Daniel Beal, *Dances from Norway* (Minneapolis: Sons of Norway, 1988), 138.

14. The process by which these newer types of tunes, also called *runddansslåtter*, were reshaped by musicians in Norway is discussed in Arvid O. Vollsnes, ed., *Norges musikkhistorie*, vol. 3, *1870–1910: Romantikk og Gullalder*, ed. Finn Benestad, Nils Grinde, and Harald Herresthal (Oslo: Aschehoug, 1999), 277, and in Olav Sæta, "Tradisjoner for vanlig fele—og en del annet" (unpublished manuscript, November 2004), 9.

15. Vollsnes, *Norges musikkhistorie*, 3:274.

16. Egil Bakka, "The Polka Before and After the Polka," *Yearbook for Traditional Music* 33 (2011): 41–42. As Bakka explains, the polka was known by several other names in different parts of Norway: *hamborgar, skotsk, hoppvals,* and *galopp.* But in Ole Hendricks's manuscript, the term *polka* appears, not the others.

17. Goertzen, *Fiddling for Norway,* 16.

18. Nusbaum, "Norwegian Traditional Music in Minnesota," 4:115; and Rue, "From Revival to Remix," 31.

19. Nusbaum, "Norwegian Traditional Music in Minnesota," 4:114.

20. Jo[h]n Stulen, "Dansemusikk for fiolin (og bass)," National Library of Norway, Mus.ms. 4689; Severin Jevnager, "Dansemusikk for fiolin," National Library of Norway, Mus.ms. 6272.

21. See Egil Bakka, *Norske dansetradisjonar* (Oslo: Norske Samlaget, 1978), 105–6, and Alix Cordray, "Dances from Norway (and a Few Other Places)."

22. M. B. Gilbert, *Round Dancing* (Portland, ME: printed by the author, 1890), 119–23.

23. Beal, *Dances from Norway,* 145–46.

24. Atle Lien Jenssen, *Gamle notebøker og opptegnelser fra Hedmarken* (Espa, Norway: Lokalhistorisk Forlag, 1992), 15–16.

25. Ole Feiring and Jon Feiring, eds., *Fra menuett til masurka: Mjøsbygdmusikk gjennom 200 år* (Gjøvik, Norway: Gjøvik Historielag, 1991), 78–79; Thomas Nilssen, notes to *Over Stok og Steen,* Over Stok og Steen, Heilo HCD7141, compact disc, 1998; Vollsnes, *Norges musikkhistorie,* 3:275.

26. Lien Jenssen, *Gamle notebøker,* 15.

27. Atle Lien Jenssen, *På Budor vi danse skar: Spelemenn og tradisjonsmusikk på Hedmarken* (Vallset, Norway: Oplandske Bokforlag, 2007), 21.

28. Alan Jabbour, "Fiddle Music," in *American Folklore: An Encyclopedia,* ed. Jan Harold Brunvand (New York: Garland, 1996), 255. Jabbour refers to titles of American fiddle tunes.

29. Thor Ola Engen, "Det er me som er Bakstadgutane: Om spellemennene Gulbrand, Peder og Hans Bakstad," *Årbok for norsk folkemusikk,* vol. 15 (Oslo: Norsk Folkemusikk- og Danselag, 2006), 63.

30. Gunhild Kolstad, *Nes bygdebok, andre bind, 2. del* (Nes, Norway: Nes Historielag, 1995), 263–64; Feiring and Feiring, *Fra menuett til masurka,* 78–79; and Lien Jenssen, *Gamle notebøker,* 17.

31. I was able to trace Thor through the following records: (1) Census record for Thor Larsen [Balstad], Nes Parish, Hedmark, Norway, 1865 (data accessed from Folketelling 1865 for 0411P Nes prestegjeld database in Digitalarkivet service of the National Archives of Norway; (2) Baptismal record for Gustava Marie Balstad [daughter of Thor Balstad], Valders and G. Jerpen Lutheran Parish, Valders,

Wisconsin, May 19, 1867 (digital image accessed from U.S. Evangelical Lutheran Church in America Church Records, 1781–1969 database on Ancestry.com); and (3) Robert A. Bjerke, *Manitowoc-skogen: A Biographical and Genealogical Directory of the Residents of Norwegian Birth and Descent in Manitowoc and Kewaunee Counties in Wisconsin from the First Settlement to 1900* (Manitowoc, WI: Dobbs, 1994), 140.

32. Nils Grinde, *A History of Norwegian Music*, trans. William H. Halverson and Leland B. Sateren (Lincoln: University of Nebraska Press, 1991), 87.

33. Sæta, *Norwegian Folk Music*, 4:63.

34. Lien Jenssen, *På Budor*, 75, 137–38; and Engen, "Det er me som er Bakstadgutane," 72–77.

35. This profile of Lars Hollo draws from Lien Jenssen, *Gamle notebøker*, 59–61; Eyvind Lillevold, *Hamars historie* ([Hamar, Norway], 1949), 488; Andreas Bjørkum, Magne Myhren, and Bjørn Aasland, eds., *Folkemusikk og folkemusikkutøvarar i Noreg 2* (Oslo: Notabene Forlag, 1996), 200; and Feiring and Feiring, *Fra menuett til masurka*, 81–82.

36. In contemporary accounts, this instrument is commonly called *waldhorn* (modern spelling: *valthorn*) and is the instrument known to English speakers as French horn (or simply, "horn"). According to Sabine Klaus, curator of brass instruments at the National Music Museum, since Sørensen played in a military band, he may have played a horn with valves (personal communication, October 19, 2018). For an example of a nineteenth-century horn with valves, see the Ringve Museum's example, catalog number RMT 665 at https://digitaltmuseum.no/011 022847442/valthorn. Note, however, that many orchestral players were still playing horns with crooks instead of valves, such as the Norsk Folkemuseum's example, catalog number NF.1904–0034A, viewable at https://digitaltmuseum.no/011 023128695/valthorn.

37. For Sørensen's biographical details, see Lars Gunhildsberg, *Anders Sørensens Danser* (Ottestad, Norway: printed by the author, 1984), 1–7; Hoksnes, *Vals til tusen*, 28–36; Lien Jenssen, *Gamle notebøker*, 17–18; and Torgeir Ziener, "Anders Sørensen," in *Store norske leksikon*, last updated February 13, 2009.

38. Gunhildsberg, *Anders Sørensens Danser*, 5. Hoksnes mentions a disastrous fire in 1904 (*Vals til tusen*, 35).

39. Thomas Nilssen, personal communication, March 4, 2019.

40. Lillevold, *Hamars historie*, 488. Spangberg's dates are derived from burial record for Martinus Nilsen Spangberg, Stange Parish, Hedmark, Norway, February 14, 1898.

41. Lien Jenssen, *Gamle notebøker*, 61.

42. Chr. Ramseth, *Hamar bys historie: Til 50 aars jubilæet, 21 mars 1899* (Hamar, Norway: L. Larsen, Axel Magnussen, H. A. Samuelsen, 1899; Hamar: Hamar Historielag, 1991), 314; Arvid Østby, *Hamar borgerbok: Litt om de første handels- og*

håndverksborgere i Hamar (Hamar: Hamar Historielag, 1998), 139; and M. Veflingstad, *Stange bygdebok*, vol. 1, *Gårds- og slektshistorien* ([Stange, Norway]: Stange Historielag, 1951), 67.

43. *Fortegnelse over matrikulerede Eiendomme og deres Skyld i Hedemarkens Amt, affattet i Henhold til Kgl. Resolution af 29de Mai og 6te December 1886*, vol. 1, *Hedemarkens Fogderi* (Kristiania, 1889), part 6, page 4, National Library of Norway; Paul Borgerdal, Lars Berg, and Olav Bryn, eds., *Norske gardsbruk: Hedmark fylke II* (Oslo: Forlaget Norske gardsbruk, 1943), 360.

44. See Marriage record for Dyre Ols Vold (Friisvold), Stange Parish, Hedmark, Norway, May 2, 1860, and Veflingstad, *Stange bygdebok*, 1:429. Dyre was the son of Ole Dyressen Friisvold and Sara Olsdatter. He married Anne Pedersdatter in 1860.

45. A record from 1854 states that Even Olsen was leaving for Christiania (Oslo) to go to brother Dyre, a *waldhorn* player working as a military musician. See out-migration record for Even Olsen, Stange Parish, Hedmark, Norway, April 15, 1854.

46. John Stulen's manuscript, "Dansemusikk for fiolin (og bass)," contains a polka "av Vold," [82]. However, it seems doubtful that D. O. Wold composed the vals in one of O. M. Sandvik's manuscripts, "Vals etter Dyre Wold, lensmann i Romedal" (see Sandvik in the bibliography). This vals may have actually been composed by Halvor Olsen Wold (1777–1827), who is the only lensmann (a minor government official) named Wold that I have found so far who also happens to have been a musician. See also Bjarne Morthoff, *Romedalboka: Garder og slekter*, vol. 2 ([Romedal, Norway]: Bygdebokkomitéen for Romedal, 1970), 87; and Lien Jenssen, *På Budor*, 72, 96–97.

47. "Obituary: D. O. Wold," *Badger State Banner*, November 14, 1912.

48. [Katharine Wesson?], "Early Trails and Roads Leading to La Crosse," handdrawn map showing roads existing during the nineteenth century, ca. 1935, University of Wisconsin Digital Collections.

49. "Obituary: D. O. Wold."

50. Karyn Marie Busby, "Dyre (David) Olssen Wold (Frisvold)," last updated August 31, 2019.

51. Thomas Nilssen, personal communication, August 16, 2018.

52. Lien Jenssen, *Gamle notebøker*, 205–7, 212; and Lien Jenssen, *På Budor*, 77, 120–21.

53. Lien Jenssen, *Gamle notebøker*, 13; Egil Bakka, *Europeisk dansehistorie: for VK 1 og VK 2* (Oslo: Gyldendal undervisning, 1997), 163.

54. Hans-Christian Arent, "Fandango," in *Store norske leksikon*, last updated June 8, 2017; Olaf Koppang, quoted in Klara Semb, *Norske folkedansar: Turdansar* (Oslo: Noregs Boklag, 1991), 50; and Ronny Kjøsen and Thomas Nilssen, notes to *Over Stok og Steen*, *Til almuen*, 2L 2L15, 2003.

55. Klara Semb, *Norske folkedansar*, vol. 2, *Rettleiing om dansen* (Oslo: Noregs Ungdomslag, 1922), 87.

56. Klara Semb, *Norske folkedansar*, vol. 2, *Rettleiing om dansen*, 5th ed. (Oslo: Noregs Boklag, 1975), 221–24, 239–41.

57. In a figaro with one mill, only one "square" (two couples) are dancing at any one time; the rest of the dancers wait in line until their turn. With two mills, two squares (a total of four couples) are dancing at a time. Examples can be viewed on YouTube, since the figaro is still danced in Norway today. The names of these dances are sometimes written as *figaro med ei mylne* and *figaro med tvo mylnor*.

58. Semb, *Norske folkedansar* (1975), 212–20.

59. Brøgger probably played a horn designed to be played with crooks and hand-stopping, such as the Norsk Folkemuseum's example, catalog number NF.19 04–0040AK.

60. Terje Bratberg, "Brøgger," in *Store norske leksikon*; A. W. Brøgger, *Slekten Brøgger: Med oplysninger om familiene Bader, Bjerring, Breda, Lem, Lie, Siewers, Ursin* (Oslo: A. W. Brøggers Boktrykkeri, 1931), 5–26; Geir Hestmark, *Vitenskap og nasjon: Waldemar Christopher Brøgger, 1851–1905* (Oslo: Aschehoug, 1999), 25.

61. I have been unable to locate any collections or anthologies containing this repertoire that were published before 1900, nor is Thomas Nilssen aware of any pre-1900 publications (personal communication, August 23, 2018).

62. Ulvestad, *Norge i Amerika med kart*, 102, 257, 390, 488, 530, and 543. Cashton, the county seat of Monroe County, Wisconsin, was home to many people from Akershus. One of the larger population groups in Warrens, Monroe County, came from Biri in Oppland.

63. According to the 1900 U.S. census, Anton Tømten immigrated with his family in 1868 at the age of thirteen (1900 United States Census, Coon, Vernon County, Wisconsin, population schedule, dwelling 46, family 46, June 5–6, 1900, digital image accessed on Ancestry.com, s.v. "Tomten, Anton"). Three tunes from Tømten's repertoire appear in Feiring and Feiring's *Fra menuett til masurka* (#390–92, p. N250). With some pride, the Feirings note that Anton became one of the most sought-after musicians in the Westby area (89–90). Many of Anton's nine children were musical, and a son and granddaughter were interviewed by Philip Martin for his profile of Anton in "Hoppwaltzes and Homebrew," 265. Martin includes a photograph of Tømten's orchestra in his *Farmhouse Fiddlers*, 27.

64. Martin, *Farmhouse Fiddlers*, 118–20; and Mary Barthelemy, personal communication, October 10, 2018.

65. Records for Samuelstad include: (1) T. Lauvdal, *Vardal bygdebok: II* (Gjøvik, Norway: printed by the author, 1930), 308; (2) 1880 United States Census, Pigeon Township, Trempealeau County, Wisconsin, population schedule, p. 5, dwelling 44, family 45, June 4, 1880 (digital image accessed on Ancestry.com, s.v. "Semulstad,

[*sic*] Hans O."); (3) Homestead Certificate no. 4451 issued April 20, 1882, to Hans O. Samuelstad by General Land Office in La Crosse, WI (digital image accessed from U.S. General Land Office Records, 1776–2015 database on Ancestry.com); and (4) Burial record for Hans O. Samuelstad, Whitehall Lutheran Church, Whitehall, Wisconsin, November 30, 1892 (digital image accessed from U.S. Evangelical Lutheran Church in America Church Records, 1781–1969 database on Ancestry .com).

66. "The Migration from Stange, Hedmark, Norway," Geni (online genealogy service), accessed August 31, 2019, https://www.geni.com/projects/The-Migration -From-Stange-Hedmark-Norway/18782; and Sæta, *Norwegian Folk Music*, 4:62. Eidskog and Kongsvinger are about eighty miles south of Hamar.

67. See Ulvestad, *Norge i Amerika*, 166, 177, 296, 425.

68. "The Migration from Stange, Hedmark, Norway."

69. Tomta's early history is traced by Eyvind Lillevold in his *Vinger bygdebok: Gards- og slektshistorie*, vol. 3, *Austmarka med Varaldskog* ([Kongsvinger, Norway: Bygdebokkomitéen], 1977), 514–15. With some difficulty, I was able to trace Andreas Tomta, who became known as Andrew Thorson after immigrating, through census records, his death record, and the Minneapolis city directories for 1882–97. He is described as a musician or music teacher in the 1895 Minnesota state census and in the city directories for 1885, 1891, and 1893–97. The actual records are: (1) 1895 Minnesota State Census, Minneapolis—Ward 3, Hennepin County, 51, June 11, 1895, data accessed from the Minnesota, Territorial and State Censuses, 1849–1905 database on Ancestry.com, s.v. "Thorson, Andrew"; (2) Minneapolis City Directory Collection, Hennepin County Library, accessed October 4, 2018; and (3) Death record for Andrew Thorson, Minneapolis, Hennepin County, Minnesota, July 2, 1912, data accessed from Minnesota Deaths and Burials, 1835–1990 database in FamilySearch.

70. Nusbaum, "Norwegian Traditional Music in Minnesota," 4:115.

71. Jamison, *Hoedowns, Reels, and Frolics*, 33–35.

72. Skiba, "Here, Everybody Dances," 224–25.

73. Beal, *Dances from Norway*, 80, 83–84; Goertzen, *Fiddling for Norway*, 16. The lanciers (lancers) and francaise, both of which are variants of the quadrille, were also danced in Norway. Feiring and Feiring's *Fra menuett til masurka* contains sets of tunes for these variants. Additional examples can be found in Lien Jenssen, *Gamle notebøker*, 40–44.

74. Many examples may be found in *An American Ballroom Companion: Dance Instruction Manuals, ca. 1490–1920* at the Library of Congress.

75. Herman A. Strassburg, *Call Book of Modern Quadrilles* (Detroit: American Music, 1889).

76. J. H. Harvey, *Wehman's Complete Dancing Master and Call Book: Containing a Full and Complete Description of all the Modern Dances, Together with the Figures of the German* (New York: Henry J. Wehman, 1889), 48.

77. F. Leslie Clendenen provides directions for three three-figure quadrilles and eight four-figure quadrilles; see *Prof. Clendenen's Fashionable Quadrille Book and Guide to Etiquette* (Davenport, IA: F. L. Clendenen, 1895), 17–24, 49, 53, and 57. See also *Squire's Practical Prompter, or, Ball Room Call Book* (Cincinnati: A. Squire, 1887), Stanford Dance website, which contains directions for ten uncomplicated quadrilles of three figures each.

78. James Kimball, personal communication, June 13, 2016; Simon J. Bronner, *Old-Time Music Makers of New York State* (Syracuse: Syracuse University Press, 1987), 65. Floyd Woodhull, one of Bronner's informants, explained that "the third [number] is generally a livelier tune, what they call a jig or a breakdown. That's when they want to cut loose, that third number."

79. "At Lake Minnetonka," *Minneapolis Tribune*, August 9, 1899.

80. "The Charity Ball," *Minneapolis Tribune*, November 5, 1898. The two-step was a very simple dance whose basic movement was a slide-close-slide. Ole might have been able to repurpose some of his quadrille tunes if obliged to play for the two-step, since it was danced to music in duple $\frac{2}{4}$ or triple $\frac{6}{8}$ time. See Susan de Guardiola, "Two-Step (circa 1900)."

81. One example is *Arling Shaeffer's Barn Dance: World's Greatest Collection of Quadrilles, Jigs, Reels and Hornpipes with All Calls* (Chicago: M. M. Cole, 1932). I am indebted to Paul Tyler for pointing out the persistence of quadrilles in rural areas: "Three 'changes' or figures were danced in many communities from the late nineteenth century well into the post–[World War II] part of the twentieth century, though some local terminologies did away with the idea that they were quadrille changes. They were simply three square dances in a 'tip'" (personal communication, February 1, 2019).

82. Some of Finseth's quadrille tunes were transcribed by Otto Rindlisbacher and are preserved in the Wisconsin Music Archives in the Mills Music Library at the University of Wisconsin–Madison.

83. Marshall, *Play Me Something Quick and Devilish*, 174.

84. Christopher Martin, "Theater," in *Oxford Encyclopedia of American Social History* (Oxford: Oxford University Press, 2012).

85. Clayton W. Henderson, "Minstrelsy, American"; and Matt Clavin, "Minstrel Shows," in *Encyclopedia of the United States in the Nineteenth Century*, ed. Paul Finkelman (New York: Charles Scribner's Sons, 2001).

86. "Town and County News," *Grant County Herald*, February 13, 1896.

87. Robert C. Toll, *Blacking Up: The Minstrel Show in Nineteenth-Century America* (New York: Oxford University Press, 1974), 211–12.

88. "Things as They Occur," *Grant County Herald*, March 4, 1897.

89. "Things as They Occur," *Grant County Herald*, January 13, 1898.

90. "Town and County News," *Grant County Herald*, February 21, 1895; and "The Minstrel Show: Elbow Lake's Colored Gentry Disport to a Large Audience," *Grant County Herald*, March 7, 1895.

91. "Town and County News," *Grant County Herald*, March 7, 1895.

92. Jevnager, "Dansemusikk for fiolin"; Stulen, "Dansemusikk for fiolin (og bass)."

93. Beth Hoven Rotto kindly allowed me to examine her copy of Johan Arndt's collection. Some of his music is featured on the Foot-Notes CD *My Father Was a Fiddler* and in Beth Hoven Rotto, *My Father Was a Fiddler Tunebook* (Decorah, IA: printed by the author, 1998).

94. Larson, "Scandinavian-American Folk Dance Music," xii and 482.

95. Robert Andresen, "Traditional Music: The Real Story of Ethnic Music and How It Evolved in Minnesota and Wisconsin," *Minnesota Monthly* 12 (October 1978): 11.

96. Janet Ann Kvam, "Norwegian-American Dance Music in Minnesota and Its Roots in Norway: A Comparative Study" (DMA diss., University of Missouri–Kansas City, 1986), 53, 61. Sjøk was referring to Severin Jevnager (1869–1928) of Elverum, Hedmark.

97. Kvam, "Norwegian-American Dance Music," 62.

98. Kvam, "Norwegian-American Dance Music," 61.

99. *Tunes from the Amerika Trunk: Traditional Norwegian-American Music from Wisconsin*, vol. 2, produced by Philip Martin, Wisconsin Folklife Center—Folklore Village Farm Records FVF 202, released 1984, 33⅓ rpm; *Norwegian-American Music from Minnesota: Old-Time and Traditional Favorites*, produced by Philip Nusbaum, Minnesota Historical Society Press, released 1989, 33⅓ rpm.

100. Mary Pat Kleven, *The Music of Elmo Wick: Fiddle Tunes of Crow River Country* (Cannon Falls, MN: printed by the author, 2016), ii.

101. Vollsnes, "Norway–Music and Musical Life," 285.

102. Robert Baron and Ana C. Cara, "Introduction: Creolization and Folklore—Cultural Creativity in Process," *Journal of American Folklore* 116, no. 459 (Winter 2003): 4–8.

103. James P. Leary, *Polkabilly: How the Goose Island Ramblers Redefined American Folk Music* (New York: Oxford University Press, 2006), 13.

104. Leary, *Polkabilly*, 9–38.

105. Andresen, "Traditional Music," 9.

A FARMER AND HIS FIDDLE IN THE NEW CENTURY

1. *Standard Atlas of Grant County, Minnesota*.

2. "Town and Country News," *Grant County Herald*, March 14, 1895; "Things as They Occur," *Grant County Herald*, March 31, 1898.

3. "Town and County News," *Grant County Herald*, June 25, 1896; July 9, 1896; and July 16, 1896.

4. "Things as They Occur," *Grant County Herald*, June 29, 1899.

5. "Things as They Occur," *Grant County Herald*, February 15, 1900.

6. "Obituary," *Grant County Herald*, July 22, 1897; "Lost Their Babe," *Grant County Herald*, September 26, 1901.

7. "Damage Great: Rust Is Raising Havoc with Grain and Hopes of a Big Crop Are Blasted," *Grant County Herald*, August 4, 1904; "Poor Potatoes," *Grant County Herald*, October 5, 1905.

8. Tammy Hendricks Creasy, personal communication, May 17, 2014.

9. Fraser, *Prairie Fires*, 165.

10. Barbara Levorsen, *The Quiet Conquest: A History of the Lives and Times of the First Settlers of Central North Dakota* (Hawley, MN: Hawley Herald, 1974), 4.

11. Ann Romines, *Constructing the Little House: Gender, Culture, and Laura Ingalls Wilder* (Amherst: University of Massachusetts Press, 1997), 44. Charles Ingalls, a fiddler, was the father of Laura Ingalls Wilder, the author of the *Little House on the Prairie* series of books for young readers. Ingalls's fiddling figures prominently in the series.

12. Rose Wilder Lane, "Grandpa's Fiddle I," in *A Little House Sampler*, ed. William T. Anderson (Lincoln: University of Nebraska Press, 1988), 68. I am indebted to Dale Cockrell for locating this passage. Rose Wilder Lane was the daughter of Laura Ingalls Wilder.

13. "Band Concert," *Grant County Herald*, July 20, 1899.

14. "Things as They Occur," *Grant County Herald*, February 16, 1899.

15. "Fair Music: A Concert by Local Talent on Wednesday and Thursday Evenings," *Grant County Herald*, September 9, 1897; "Turn of the Tide," *Grant County Herald*, December 23, 1897.

16. "Turn of the Tide," *Grant County Herald*, December 23, 1897; "Things as They Occur," *Grant County Herald*, October 19, 1899, and August 23, 1900. Albert's out-of-town musical engagements are mentioned in numerous issues of the *Herald* (e.g., July 6, 1899, and July 4, 1901).

17. "Bits of Local Information," *Grant County Herald*, November 24, 1910.

18. "Bits of Local Information," *Grant County Herald*, September 1, 1910.

19. "Bits of Local Information," *Grant County Herald*, March 23, 1911.

20. News item, *Grant County Herald*, August 19, 1909.

21. "Grasshoppers Are Busy," *Grant County Herald*, September 2, 1909.

22. "Crop Situation Serious" and "Hay Crop Short," *Grant County Herald*, July 14, 1910.

23. Larson, "Scandinavian-American Folk Dance Music," 2–3.

24. Qualey and Gjerde, "The Norwegians," 223–24, 229.

25. Martin, *Farmhouse Fiddlers*, 83–91.

26. "Cambridge," *North Star* (Cambridge, MN), September 13, 1917.

27. "Veteran Fiddlers Recall Days of the Old Round Dances and Dance Calls," *Minneapolis Morning Tribune*, February 15, 1914.

28. Martin, *Farmhouse Fiddlers*, 96. Victor Greene explores the golden age of ethnic old-time entertainers (ca. 1914 through the 1950s) in *A Passion for Polka*.

29. Chris Goertzen, *Southern Fiddlers and Fiddle Contests* (Jackson: University Press of Mississippi, 2008), 8.

30. Guthrie Meade, "Fiddle Contests in Minnesota and Wisconsin in 1926," unpublished survey of newspaper articles, Robert Andresen Collection (Series I: Manuscript Files, Subseries: Scandinavian Files, Folder 5: Early Minnesota and Wisconsin Fiddler Contests), Mills Music Library, University of Wisconsin–Madison; Martin, "Hoppwaltzes and Homebrew," 259; and James P. Leary and Richard March, *Down Home Dairyland: A Listener's Guide* (Madison, WI: Center for Study of Upper Midwestern Cultures, 2004), 13–15. Many writers have stated that these contests were instigated and sponsored by the automobile tycoon Henry Ford. Paul M. Gifford came to a different conclusion after his extensive archival research into Ford's efforts to revive old-time music and dance ("Henry Ford's Dance Revival and Fiddle Contests: Myth and Reality," *Journal of the Society for American Music* 4, no. 3 [2010]: 307–38). The first contest was sponsored by the managers of certain Ford dealerships in Kentucky, Indiana, and Tennessee. According to Gifford, Ford's interests may have inspired the first and subsequent contests, but he never sponsored any of them: "The number and variety of contests became so large that Ford and his staff simply decided to avoid involvement in any of them" (329). One active promoter of fiddle contests in the Upper Midwest was William Mitchell, whose unpublished scrapbook is preserved at the Mills Music Library. (Ole Hendricks does not seem to have competed in any of Mitchell's contests.) See W[illiam] Mitchell, Fiddlers contest scrapbook, Lanesboro, MN, ca. 1927–28, Local Centers/Global Sounds: Historic Recordings and Midwestern Musical Vernaculars, University of Wisconsin Digital Collections.

31. Lorena A. Hickok, "Old-Timers Will Cross Bows for Fiddler's Crown Tonight," *Minneapolis Morning Tribune*, February 5, 1926.

32. "Many Hear Old-Time Fiddlers in Contest," *North Star* (Cambridge, MN), February 11, 1926. The article gives Ole's age as seventy-six, inflating his age by one year. Ole might have believed he was born in 1850, as it was not unusual for immigrants to forget their exact age. His parents, like Norwegians of their generation, probably calculated age by a person's *next* birthday, rather than his or her *last* birthday, and this might have led to confusion about Ole's birth year (Jim Hove, personal communication, February 10, 2016). One of the fifteen semifinalists actually withdrew, leaving fourteen fiddlers in that round (Lorena A. Hickok, "'King Tut,' Fiddling Pharaoh, Wins Northwest Championship," *Minneapolis Morning Tribune*,

February 6, 1926). Ole's final standing after the semifinals ("about eighth") was approximate presumably due to the nature of the judging based on audience applause.

About this Edition

1. Jim Hove, personal communication, August 8, 2016.
2. James Kimball, personal communication, July 13, 2016.
3. Dale Cockrell, ed., *The Ingalls Wilder Family Songbook*, Recent Researches in American Music, vol. 71 (Middleton, WI: A-R Editions, 2011), 343.
4. Larson, "Scandinavian-American Folk Dance Music," 60.

The Transcriptions

1. "Durang, John," in *The Oxford Companion to American Theatre*, 3rd ed., ed. Gerald Bordman and Thomas S. Hischak.
2. Michael Broyles, "Immigrant, Folk, and Regional Musics in the Nineteenth Century," in *The Cambridge History of American Music* (Cambridge: Cambridge University Press, 1998), 143–44.
3. Samuel P. Bayard, *Dance to the Fiddle, March to the Fife: Instrumental Folk Tunes in Pennsylvania* (University Park: Pennsylvania State University Press, 1982), 344; Jamison, *Hoedowns, Reels, and Frolics*, 251.
4. Jeffrey J. Noonan, *The Guitar in America: Victorian Era to Jazz Age* (Jackson: University Press of Mississippi, 2008), 29.
5. Tim Brooks, *Lost Sounds: Blacks and the Birth of the Recording Industry, 1890–1919* (Urbana: University of Illinois Press, 2004), 27–28. Brooks's entire chapter about Johnson (13–71) is a fascinating story.
6. Egil Bakka, "Engelskdans," in *Cappelens musikkleksikon*, ed. Kari Michelsen (Oslo: J. W. Cappelens Forlag, 1978), 2:387.
7. Thomas F. DeFrantz, "Duke University Professor Thomas F. DeFrantz: Buck, Wing and Jig," YouTube video, 2:50, March 26, 2012.
8. Pauline Norton, "Buck and Wing," in Grove Music Online, published February 23, 2011.
9. "The Dancing School at Palace Opera House, Wednesday Eve., Jan. 27," *Record and Union* (Rochester, MN), January 22, 1886.
10. Brøgger, *Slekten Brøgger*, 24.
11. Feiring and Feiring, *Fra menuett til masurka*, 74–77. Lien Jenssen reproduced the contents of Midtlien's manuscript, "Gamle danse og gamle musikere," dated 1930, in *Gamle notebøker* (33–39) and in *På Budor* (295–304).
12. William H. Rehrig, *The Heritage Encyclopedia of Band Music: Composers and Their Music*, ed. Paul E. Bierley (Westerville, OH: Integrity, 1991–96), 1:218 and 2:801.
13. Rehrig, *Heritage Encyclopedia of Band Music*, 2:845.
14. Jevnager, "Dansemusikk for fiolin," #56, #96–98, and #223.

Bibliography

"12 Danser af L. Holo." 1872. National Library of Norway, Mus.ms.a 1981. https:// urn.nb.no/URN:NBN:no-nb_digimanus_316487.

An American Ballroom Companion: Dance Instruction Manuals, ca. 1490 to 1920. Accessed August 22, 2019. https://www.loc.gov/collections/dance-instruction -manuals-from-1490-to-1920/about-this-collection/.

American Vernacular Music Manuscripts, ca. 1730–1910: Digital Collections from the American Antiquarian Society and the Center for Popular Music. Center for Popular Music, Middle Tennessee State University. Accessed August 19, 2019. http://popmusic.mtsu.edu/ManuscriptMusic/.

Andresen, Robert. "Traditional Music: The Real Story of Ethnic Music and How It Evolved in Minnesota and Wisconsin." *Minnesota Monthly* 12 (October 1978): 9–13.

Arent, Hans-Christian. "Fandango." In *Store norske leksikon.* Last updated June 8, 2017. https://snl.no/fandango.

Arndt, Johan. Manuscript of fiddle tunes. Collection of Beth Hoven Rotto.

"At Lake Minnetonka." *Minneapolis Tribune,* August 9, 1899. Minnesota Digital Newspaper Hub. http://www.mnhs.org/newspapers/lccn/sn83016771/1899-08 -09/ed-1/seq-5.

Atlas and Farmers' Directory of Isanti County, Minnesota: Containing Plats of All Townships with Owners Names. St. Paul: Webb, 1914.

Avery, Patricia Jo Kinman. "An Investigation of Music Education Rudiments in Selected American Tunebooks of the Eighteenth and Nineteenth Century: 1700 to 1900." DMA diss., Shenandoah University, 2001. ProQuest Dissertations & Theses Global (3060350).

Bakka, Egil. "Engelskdans." In *Cappelens musikkleksikon,* edited by Kari Michelsen, 2:387. Oslo: J. W. Cappelens Forlag, 1978.

Bakka, Egil. *Europeisk dansehistorie: for VK 1 og VK 2.* Oslo: Gyldendal under- visning, 1997.

Bakka, Egil. *Norske dansetradisjonar.* Oslo: Norske Samlaget, 1978.

Bakka, Egil. "The Polka Before and After the Polka." *Yearbook for Traditional Music* 33 (2011): 37–47.

Baron, Robert, and Ana C. Cara. "Introduction: Creolization and Folklore— Cultural Creativity in Process." *Journal of American Folklore* 116, no. 459 (Winter 2003): 4–8.

Bayard, Samuel P. *Dance to the Fiddle, March to the Fife: Instrumental Folk Tunes in Pennsylvania.* University Park: Pennsylvania State University Press, 1982.

Beal, Daniel. *Dances from Norway.* Minneapolis: Sons of Norway, 1988.

Bjerke, Robert A. *Manitowoc-skogen: A Biographical and Genealogical Directory of the Residents of Norwegian Birth and Descent in Manitowoc and Kewaunee Counties in Wisconsin from the First Settlement to 1900.* Manitowoc, WI: Dobbs, 1994. https://www.rbjerke.net/books/manitowoc-skogen/.

Bjørkum, Andreas, Magne Myhren, and Bjørn Aasland, eds. *Folkemusikk og folkemusikkutøvarar i Noreg 2.* Oslo: Notabene Forlag, 1996.

Borgerdal, Paul, Lars Berg, and Olav Bryn, eds. *Norske gardsbruk: Hedmark fylke II.* Oslo: Forlaget Norske gardsbruk, 1943.

Bratberg, Terje. "Brøgger." In *Store norske leksikon.* Last updated February 4, 2009. https://snl.no/Brøgger.

Brøgger, A. W. *Slekten Brøgger: Med oplysninger om familiene Bader, Bjerring, Breda, Lem, Lie, Siewers, Ursin.* Oslo: A. W. Brøggers Boktrykkeri, 1931.

Bronner, Simon J. *Old-Time Music Makers of New York State.* Syracuse: Syracuse University Press, 1987.

Brooks, Tim. *Lost Sounds: Blacks and the Birth of the Recording Industry, 1890–1919.* Urbana: University of Illinois Press, 2004.

Broyles, Michael. "Immigrant, Folk, and Regional Musics in the Nineteenth Century." In *The Cambridge History of American Music,* 135–57. Cambridge: Cambridge University Press, 1998.

Busby, Karyn Marie. "Dyre (David) Olssen Wold (Frisvold)." Last updated August 31, 2019. https://www.geni.com/people/Dyhre-Wold/6000000014085258923.

"Cambridge." *North Star* (Cambridge, MN), September 13, 1917. Accessed at the Minnesota Historical Society.

"The Charity Ball." *Minneapolis Tribune,* November 5, 1898. Minnesota Digital Newspaper Hub. http://www.mnhs.org/newspapers/lccn/sn83016771/1898-11-05/ed-1/seq-8.

Christeson, R. P. *The Old-Time Fiddler's Repertory: 245 Traditional Tunes.* Columbia: University of Missouri Press, 1973.

Clavin, Matt. "Minstrel Shows." In *Encyclopedia of the United States in the Nineteenth Century,* edited by Paul Finkelman. New York: Charles Scribner's Sons, 2001. Credo Reference Database.

Clendenen, F. Leslie. *Prof. Clendenen's Fashionable Quadrille Book and Guide to Etiquette.* Davenport, IA: F. L. Clendenen, 1895. Library of Congress. https://www.loc.gov/item/05029176/.

Cockrell, Dale, ed. *The Ingalls Wilder Family Songbook.* Recent Researches in American Music 71. Middleton, WI: A-R Editions, 2011.

Cordray, Alix. "Dances from Norway (and a Few Other Places)." Alix Cordray website. Accessed December 30, 2019. https://www.cordray.no/Norwegian Dances/201303-Dances.html.

Cordray, Alix. "Survey of Norwegian Dance." Alix Cordray website. Accessed July 14, 2019. https://www.cordray.no/NorwegianDances/Dances/Survey-Mendocino -2015.pdf.

Correct Map of Dakota Compiled from United States and Territorial Surveys, Nov. 1, 1882. Chicago: Rand McNally, 1882. Library of Congress, Geography and Map Division. https://hdl.loc.gov/loc.gmd/g4181p.rr003700.

Crandall, Horace B. *A History of Richland County: Its Geographical Boundaries, Township Organizations, Soil, Improved and Unimproved Lands, Early Settlers, Leading Farmers, Bonanza Farms, County Officers, City and Town Officers, Professions, Business Firms, Mechanical Industries, Schools, Churches, Benevolent Societies, Public Improvements, Railroad Advantages, Etc., Etc.* Colfax, Dakota Territory: printed by the author, 1886. Hathi Trust Digital Library. https://hdl.handle.net/2027/loc.ark:/13960/t00z7hr24.

"Dance Forms." Hardanger Fiddle Association of America. Accessed July 14, 2019. http://www.hfaa.org/Home/Dances.

"Dansemusikk; Fiolinmusikk." National Library of Norway, Mus.ms. 4785. https://urn.nb.no/URN:NBN:no-nb_digimanus_174801. Compilers of this manuscript (dated 1861, 1876–78) include E. J. Foss and Eduard Gustvedt.

"The Dancing School at Palace Opera House, Wednesday Eve., Jan. 27." *Record and Union* (Rochester, MN), January 22, 1886. Minnesota Digital Newspaper Hub, http://www.mnhs.org/newspapers/lccn/sn85025572/1886-01-22/ed-1/seq-3.

De Guardiola, Susan. "Two-Step (circa 1900)." Capering & Kickery blog. Accessed August 24, 2018. http://www.kickery.com/two-step-circa-1900/.

DeFrantz, Thomas F. "Duke University Professor Thomas F. DeFrantz: Buck, Wing and Jig." YouTube video, 2:50. March 26, 2012. https://youtu.be/A34OD 4eA170.

Devere, Sam. *The Whistling Coon.* New York: William A. Pond, ca. 1888. Francis G. Spencer Collection of American Popular Sheet Music, Baylor University Digital Collections. https://digitalcollections-baylor.quartexcollections.com/Documents/Detail/whistling-coon/123590.

Dick's Quadrille Call-book and Ball-Room Prompter. New York: Fitzgerald Publishing, 1895. Hathi Trust Digital Library. https://hdl.handle.net/2027/iau.3185804 6822106.

"Durang, John." In *The Oxford Companion to American Theatre*, 3rd ed., edited by Gerald Bordman and Thomas S. Hischak. Oxford Reference database. Last updated 2012. https://oxfordreference.com.

Emmel, H. *6th Lancers–Annette*. Arranged by E. C. Walston. Philadelphia: J. W. Pepper, 1882. Library of Congress. https://www.loc.gov/item/sm1882.20985/.

Engen, Thor Ola. "Det er me som er Bakstadgutane: Om spellemennene Gulbrand, Peder og Hans Bakstad." In *Årbok for norsk folkemusikk*, vol. 15, 63–77. Oslo: Norsk Folkemusikk- og Danselag, 2006.

Fapso, Richard J. *Norwegians in Wisconsin*. Rev. ed. Madison: Wisconsin Historical Society Press, 2001.

Feiring, Ole, and Jon Feiring, eds. *Fra menuett til masurka: Mjøsbygdmusikk gjennom 200 år*. Gjøvik, Norway: Gjøvik Historielag, 1991.

Fite, Gilbert C. *The Farmers' Frontier, 1865–1900*. New York: Holt, Rinehart and Winston, 1966.

Ford, Ira W. *Traditional Music of America*. New York: E. P. Dutton, 1940. Reprint, Hatboro, PA: Folklore Associates, 1965.

Fortegnelse over matrikulerede Eiendomme og deres Skyld i Hedemarkens Amt, affattet i Henhold til Kgl. Resolution af 29de Mai og 6te December 1886. Vol. 1, *Hedemarkens Fogderi*. Kristiania, 1889. National Library of Norway. https://urn.nb.no/URN:NBN:no-nb_digibok_2012091905035.

Fraser, Caroline. *Prairie Fires: The American Dreams of Laura Ingalls Wilder*. New York: Metropolitan Books, 2017.

Gaukstad, Øystein, and Bjørn Aksdal. "Myllarguten." In *Store norske leksikon*. Last updated December 11, 2019. https://snl.no/Myllarguten.

Gifford, Paul M. "Henry Ford's Dance Revival and Fiddle Contests: Myth and Reality." *Journal of the Society for American Music* 4, no. 3 (2010): 307–38.

Gilbert, M. B. *Round Dancing*. Portland, ME: printed by the author, 1890. Library of Congress. https://www.loc.gov/item/05029201/.

Goertzen, Chris. *Fiddling for Norway: Revival and Identity*. Chicago: University of Chicago Press, 1997.

Goertzen, Chris. *George P. Knauff's Virginia Reels and the History of American Fiddling*. Jackson: University Press of Mississippi, 2017.

Goertzen, Chris. *Southern Fiddlers and Fiddle Contests*. Jackson: University Press of Mississippi, 2008.

Goetzinger, Bill. *Elbow Lake: The First 100 Years, 1887–1987*. Elbow Lake, MN: Elbow Lake Centennial Committee, 1987.

Greene, Victor. *A Passion for Polka: Old-Time Ethnic Music in America*. Berkeley: University of California Press, 1992.

Grinde, Nils. *A History of Norwegian Music*. Translated by William H. Halverson and Leland B. Sateren. Lincoln: University of Nebraska Press, 1991.

Gunhildsberg, Lars. *Anders Sørensens Danser*. Ottestad, Norway: printed by the author, 1984.

Hammer, Kenneth M. "Come to God's Country: Promotional Efforts in Dakota Territory, 1861–1889." *South Dakota History* 10, no. 4 (Fall 1980): 291–309. https://www.sdhspress.com/journal/south-dakota-history-10-4/.

Hanssen, K. J. *Dans! Ropte Fela! 15 Norske folkdanse udsatte for en og to violiner*. 7 vols. Kristiania: Haakon Zapffe, 1902–7.

Harvey, J. H. *Wehman's Complete Dancing Master and Call Book: Containing a Full and Complete Description of All the Modern Dances, Together with the Figures of the German*. New York: Henry J. Wehman, 1889. Library of Congress. https://www.loc.gov/item/musdi.091/.

Haugen, Anders. "Manuskripten: Danse af Anders Sörensen for fiolin." National Library of Norway, Mus.ms.a 2715. https://urn.nb.no/URN:NBN:no-nb_digi manus_271785.

Haugen, Einar, and Camilla Cai. *Ole Bull: Norway's Romantic Musician and Cosmopolitan Patriot*. Madison: University of Wisconsin Press, 1993.

Henderson, Clayton W. "Minstrelsy, American." *Grove Music Online*. Published 2001. https://doi.org/10.1093/gmo/9781561592630.article.18749.

Henley, William. *Universal Dictionary of Violin and Bow Makers*. Brighton, UK: Amati Publishing, 1973.

Hestmark, Geir. *Vitenskap og nasjon: Waldemar Christopher Brøgger, 1851–1905*. Oslo: Aschehoug, 1999.

Hickok, Lorena A. "'King Tut,' Fiddling Pharaoh, Wins Northwest Championship." *Minneapolis Morning Tribune*, February 6, 1926. Accessed at the Minnesota Historical Society.

Hickok, Lorena A. "Old-Timers Will Cross Bows for Fiddler's Crown Tonight." *Minneapolis Morning Tribune*, February 5, 1926. Accessed at the Minnesota Historical Society.

Hoksnes, Arild. *Vals til tusen: Gammaldansmusikken gjennom 200 år*. Oslo: Norske Samlaget, 1988.

Howe, Elias, Jr. *American Dancing Master and Ball-Room Prompter*. Boston: Elias Howe, 1866. Hathi Trust Digital Library. https://hdl.handle.net/2027/nyp.334 33010696080.

Howe, Elias, Jr. *First Part of the Musician's Companion: Containing 18 Setts of Cotillions Arranged with Figures, and a Large Number of Popular Marches, Quick-Steps, Waltzes, Hornpipes, Contra Dances, Songs, &c. &c.* Boston: Oliver Ditson, [1850]. Internet Archive. https://archive.org/details/firstthirdpartofo1howe.

Howe, Elias, Jr. *The Musician's Omnibus*. 4 vols. Boston: Elias Howe, 1863–69. IMSLP: Petrucci Music Library. https://imslp.org/wiki/Musician's_Omnibus_ (Howe%2C_Elias).

Howe, Elias, Jr. *The Pianist's Social Circle: A Collection of Vocal and Instrumental Music for the Piano-Forte*. Boston: Elias Howe, 1869. Internet Archive. https://archive.org/details/B20899804.

Howe, Elias, Jr. *Second Part of the Musician's Companion: Containing 36 Setts of Cotillions Arranged with Figures, and a Large Number of Marches, Quick-Steps, Waltzes, Hornpipes, Contra Dances, Songs, &c. &c.* Boston: Elias Howe, 1843. Internet Archive. https://archive.org/details/secondpartofmusi02howe.

Howe, Elias, Jr. *Third Part of the Musician's Companion: Containing 40 Setts of Cotillions Arranged with Figures, and a Large Number of Popular Marches, Quick-Steps, Waltzes, Hornpipes, Contra Dances, Songs, &c. &c.* Boston: Elias Howe, 1844. Internet Archive. https://archive.org/details/thirdpartofmusic03howe.

Illustrated Souvenir of Grant County. Elbow Lake, MN: Grant County Herald, 1896.

Jabbour, Alan. "Fiddle Music." In *American Folklore: An Encyclopedia*, edited by Jan Harold Brunvand, 253–56. New York: Garland, 1996.

Jalovec, Karel. *Encyclopedia of Violin-Makers*. 2 vols. London: Paul Hamlyn, 1968.

Jamison, Phil. *Hoedowns, Reels, and Frolics: Roots and Branches of Southern Appalachian Dance*. Champaign: University of Illinois Press, 2015.

Jevnager, Severin. "Dansemusikk for fiolin." National Library of Norway, Mus. ms. 6272. https://urn.nb.no/URN:NBN:no-nb_digimanus_174820.

Kirkeby, Birger. *Bygdebok for Sauherad: Gards- og Ættesoge*. 5 vols. Sauherad, Norway: Sauherad Kommune, 1980–1988.

Kjøk, Knut. *Slåtte og leikje: Eit spelmannsrepertoar og någå attåt*. 6 vols. Oslo: Forlag 1, 2012.

Kleven, Mary Pat. *The Music of Elmo Wick: Fiddle Tunes of Crow River Country*. Cannon Falls, MN: printed by the author, 2016.

Kolstad, Gunhild. *Nes bygdebok, andre bind, 2. del*. Nes, Norway: Nes Historielag, 1995.

Kuntz, Andrew. *The Fiddler's Companion: A Descriptive Index of North American, British Isles and Irish Music for the Folk Violin and Other Instruments*. 1996–2010. http://www.ibiblio.org/fiddlers/.

Kuntz, Andrew, and Valerio Pelliccioni. The Traditional Tune Archive. https://www.tunearch.org/wiki/TTA.

Kvam, Janet Ann. "Norwegian-American Dance Music in Minnesota and Its Roots in Norway: A Comparative Study." DMA diss., University of Missouri–Kansas City, 1986. ProQuest Dissertations & Theses Global (8800638).

Lahren, Margareth Olson. *A History of Walcott, North Dakota*. [Wahpeton, ND]: Richland County Historical Society, 1975.

Lane, Rose Wilder. "Grandpa's Fiddle I." In *A Little House Sampler*, edited by William T. Anderson, 60–75. Lincoln: University of Nebraska Press, 1988.

Lansing, G[eorge] L. *The Darkie's Dream*. Boston: L. B. Gatcomb, 1891. The Lester S. Levy Sheet Music Collection. https://levysheetmusic.mse.jhu.edu/collec tion/170/101.

Larson, LeRoy Wilbur. "Scandinavian-American Folk Dance Music of the Norwegians in Minnesota." PhD diss., University of Minnesota, 1975. ProQuest Dissertations & Theses Global (7521062).

Lauvdal, T. *Vardal bygdebok: II*. Gjøvik, Norway: printed by the author, 1930.

Leary, James P. *Polkabilly: How the Goose Island Ramblers Redefined American Folk Music*. New York: Oxford University Press, 2006.

Leary, James P., and Richard March. *Down Home Dairyland: A Listener's Guide*. Madison, WI: Center for Study of Upper Midwestern Cultures, 2004.

Legreid, Ann Marie. "Community Building, Conflict, and Change: Geographic Perspectives on the Norwegian-American Experience in Frontier Wisconsin." In *Wisconsin Land and Life*, edited by Robert C. Ostergren and Thomas R. Vale, 300–319. Madison: University of Wisconsin Press, 1997.

Levorsen, Barbara. *The Quiet Conquest: A History of the Lives and Times of the First Settlers of Central North Dakota*. Hawley, MN: Hawley Herald, 1974.

Lien Jenssen, Atle. *Gamle notebøker og opptegnelser fra Hedmarken*. Espa, Norway: Lokalhistorisk Forlag, 1992.

Lien Jenssen, Atle. *På Budor vi danse skar: Spelemenn og tradisjonsmusikk på Hedmarken*. Vallset, Norway: Oplandske Bokforlag, 2007.

Lillevold, Eyvind. *Hamars historie*. [Hamar], 1949.

Lillevold, Eyvind. *Vinger bygdebok: Gards- og slektshistorie*. Vol. 3, *Austmarka med Varaldskog*. [Kongsvinger, Norway: Bygdebokkomitéen], 1977.

Lindberg, Duane R. "Pastors, Prohibition and Politics: The Role of Norwegian Clergy in the North Dakota Abstinence Movement, 1880–1920." *North Dakota Quarterly* 49 (Autumn 1981): 21–38. Hathi Trust Digital Library. https://hdl .handle.net/2027/mdp.39015038096270.

Lovoll, Odd S. *Across the Deep Blue Sea: The Saga of Early Norwegian Immigrants*. St. Paul: Minnesota Historical Society Press, 2015.

Lovoll, Odd S. *Norwegians on the Prairie: Ethnicity and the Development of the Country Town*. St. Paul: Minnesota Historical Society Press in cooperation with the Norwegian-American Historical Association, 2006.

Lowell, B. Lindsay. "The Scandinavians." In *Encyclopedia of American Social History*, edited by Mary Kupiec Cayton, Elliott J. Gorn, and Peter W. Williams, 2:701–9. New York: Charles Scribner's Sons, 1993.

"Many Hear Old-Time Fiddlers in Contest." *North Star* (Cambridge, MN), February 11, 1926. Accessed at the Minnesota Historical Society.

"Map of Monroe County." In *Historical Atlas of Wisconsin, Embracing Complete State and County Maps, City & Village Plats, Together with Separate State and*

County Histories, 70. Milwaukee: Snyder, Van Vechten, 1878. David Rumsey Map Collection at Stanford University Libraries. https://purl.stanford.edu/rk 025vp9826.

Map of Monroe County, Wisconsin. Red Wing, MN: Warner & Foot, 1877. New York Public Library Digital Collections. https://digitalcollections.nypl.org/items/c90 51e10-e512-0135-125e-6d96fb67d7bb.

Map of the La Crosse and Milwaukee Rail Road and Connections. New York: J. H. Colton, 1855. Library of Congress Geography and Map Division. https://www .loc.gov/item/98688691/.

Marshall, Howard Wight. *Play Me Something Quick and Devilish: Old-Time Fiddlers in Missouri.* Columbia: University of Missouri Press, 2012.

Martin, Christopher. "Theater." In *Oxford Encyclopedia of American Social History.* Oxford: Oxford University Press, 2012. Oxford Reference database. Last updated 2013. https://oxfordreference.com.

Martin, Philip. *Farmhouse Fiddlers: Music and Dance Traditions in the Rural Midwest.* Mount Horeb, WI: Midwest Traditions, 1994.

Martin, Philip. "Hoppwaltzes and Homebrew: Traditional Norwegian American Music from Wisconsin." In *Wisconsin Folklore*, edited by James P. Leary, 259– 67. Madison: University of Wisconsin Press, 1998.

Meade, Guthrie. "Fiddle Contests in Minnesota and Wisconsin in 1926." Unpublished survey of newspaper articles. Robert Andresen Collection. Series I: Manuscript Files, Subseries: Scandinavian Files, Folder 5: Early Minnesota and Wisconsin Fiddler Contests. Mills Music Library, University of Wisconsin–Madison.

Meyer, Sabine N. *We Are What We Drink: The Temperance Battle in Minnesota.* Urbana: University of Illinois Press, 2015.

"The Migration from Stange, Hedmark, Norway." Geni (online genealogy service). Accessed August 31, 2019. https://www.geni.com/projects/The-Migration-From -Stange-Hedmark-Norway/18782.

Minneapolis City Directory Collection. Hennepin County Library. Accessed October 4, 2018. https://box2.nmtvault.com/Hennepin2/.

Mitchell, W[illiam]. Fiddlers contest scrapbook, Lanesboro, MN, ca. 1927–28. Local Centers/Global Sounds: Historic Recordings and Midwestern Musical Vernaculars, University of Wisconsin Digital Collections. http://digital.library.wisc .edu/1711.dl/LocalCenters.FiddlersScrapbk.

Monroe County Bicentennial Committee. *Monroe County, Wisconsin, Pictorial History, 1976.* Tomah, WI: Tomah Journal, 1976.

Monroe County Marriage Records Index (1854–1968). Accessed November 2, 2018. Monroe County Local History Room and Museum. http://monroecounty history.org.

Morthoff, Bjarne. *Romedalboka: Garder og slekter.* Vol. 2. [Romedal, Norway]: Bygdebokkomitéen for Romedal, 1970.

Myhren, Magne. "Lars Fykerud." In *Store norske leksikon.* Last updated February 13, 2009. https://nbl.snl.no/Lars_Fykerud.

Noonan, Jeffrey J. *The Guitar in America: Victorian Era to Jazz Age.* Jackson: University Press of Mississippi, 2008.

Norton, Pauline. "Buck and Wing." In Grove Music Online. Published February 23, 2011. https://www.oxfordmusiconline.com/grovemusic/view/10.1093/gmo/9781561592630.001.0001/omo-9781561592630-e-1002092356.

Nusbaum, Philip. "Norwegian Traditional Music in Minnesota." In *American Musical Traditions,* edited by Jeff Todd Titon and Bob Carlin, 4:112–16. New York: Schirmer Reference, 2002.

"Obituary: D. O. Wold." *Badger State Banner,* November 14, 1912. Wisconsin Newspaper Archive–Historical Newspapers.

O'Neill, Francis. *O'Neill's Music of Ireland: Eighteen Hundred and Fifty Melodies.* Chicago: Lyon & Healy, 1903. IMSLP: Petrucci Music Library. https://imslp.org/wiki/Music_of_Ireland_(O%27Neill,_Francis)#IMSLP495828.

Østby, Arvid. *Hamar borgerbok: Litt om de første handels- og håndverksborgere i Hamar.* Hamar: Hamar Historielag, 1998.

Qualey, Carlton C., and Jon A. Gjerde. "The Norwegians." In *They Chose Minnesota: A Survey of the State's Ethnic Groups,* edited by June Drenning Holmquist, 220–47. St. Paul: Minnesota Historical Society Press, 1981.

Ramseth, Chr. *Hamar bys historie: Til 50 aars jubilæet, 21 mars 1899.* Hamar, Norway: L. Larsen, Axel Magnussen, H.A. Samuelsen, 1899. Reprint, Hamar: Hamar Historielag, 1991.

Rehrig, William H. *The Heritage Encyclopedia of Band Music: Composers and Their Music,* edited by Paul E. Bierley. 3 vols. Westerville, OH: Integrity, 1991–96.

Richards, Randolph A., ed. *History of Monroe County, Wisconsin: Past and Present, Including an Account of the Cities, Towns and Villages of the County.* Chicago: C. F. Cooper, 1912. Reprint, Evansville, IN: Unigraphic, 1977.

Rivers, C. H. *A Full Description of Modern Dances.* Brooklyn, NY [1885]. Library of Congress. https://www.loc.gov/item/05029717/.

Romines, Ann. *Constructing the Little House: Gender, Culture, and Laura Ingalls Wilder.* Amherst: University of Massachusetts Press, 1997.

Rotto, Beth Hoven. *My Father Was a Fiddler Tunebook.* Decorah, IA: printed by the author, 1998.

Rue, Anna C. "From Revival to Remix: Norwegian American Folk Music and Song." PhD diss., University of Wisconsin–Madison, 2014. ProQuest Dissertations & Theses Global (3610076).

"Russian Model Violin." National Museum of American History website. Accessed October 30, 2018. https://americanhistory.si.edu/collections/search/object/nmah_605536.

Ryan, William Bradbury. *Ryan's Mammoth Collection: 1050 Reels and Jigs, Hornpipes, Clogs, Walk-Arounds, Essences, Strathspeys, Highland Flings, and Contra Dances, with Figures, and How to Play Them.* Boston: Elias Howe, 1883. Reprinted with introduction and notes by Patrick Sky. Pacific, MO: Mel Bay Publications, 1995.

Sæta, Olav. "Fra halling til reinlender: Historisk skisse av runddansens / gammaldansens inntog i norske danse- og instrumentaltradisjoner." Unpublished manuscript, last updated November 24, 2010. https://www.uio.no/studier/emner/hf/imv/MUS1301/vii/undervisningsmateriale/Frahalling.pdf.

Sæta, Olav, ed. *Norwegian Folk Music, Series II: Slåtter for the Normal Fiddle.* Vol. 4, *Hedmark.* Oslo: Universitetsforlaget, 1997. https://urn.nb.no/URN:NBN:no-nb_digibok_2010052003088.

Sæta, Olav. "Tradisjoner for vanlig fele—og en del annet." Unpublished manuscript, November 2004. https://www.uio.no/studier/emner/hf/imv/MUS1301/vii/undervisningsmateriale/Vanligfele.pdf.

Sandvik, O. M. *Anders Sørensens danser.* Oslo: Norsk Notestik og Forlag, 1927. Sandvik's personal copy, with his corrections and additions, is available from the National Library of Norway, Mus.ms.a 2717. https://urn.nb.no/URN:NBN:no-nb_digimanus_291900.

Sandvik, O. M. "Lars Hollo: Danser." National Library of Norway, Mus.ms.a 1847. https://urn.nb.no/URN:NBN:no-nb_digimanus_293296.

Sandvik, O. M. "Slåtter og danser fra Elverums-traktene." National Library of Norway, Mus.ms.a 1814. https://urn.nb.no/URN:NBN:no-nb_digimanus_273485.

Sandvik, O. M. "Vals etter Dyre Wold, lensmann i Romedal." National Library of Norway, Mus.ms.a 1844. https://urn.nb.no/URN:NBN:no-nb_digimanus_293288.

Semb, Klara. *Norske folkedansar.* Vol. 2, *Rettleiing om dansen.* Oslo: Noregs Ungdomslag, 1922.

Semb, Klara. *Norske folkedansar.* Vol. 2, *Rettleiing om dansen.* 5th ed. Oslo: Noregs Boklag, 1975.

Semb, Klara. *Norske folkedansar: Turdansar.* Oslo: Noregs Boklag, 1991. https://urn.nb.no/URN:NBN:no-nb_digibok_2007111904027.

Shaeffer, Arling. *Arling Shaeffer's Barn Dance: World's Greatest Collection of Quadrilles, Jigs, Reels and Hornpipes with All Calls.* Chicago: M. M. Cole, 1932.

Skiba, Bob. "Here, Everybody Dances: Social Dancing in Early Minnesota." *Minnesota History* 55 (Spring 1997): 217–27. https://collections.mnhs.org/MNHistoryMagazine/articles/55/v55i05p217-227.pdf.

Squire's Practical Prompter, or, Ball Room Call Book. Cincinnati: A. Squire, 1887. Stanford Dance website. https://socialdance.stanford.edu/Syllabi/1887_Squire .PDF.

Standard Atlas of Grant County, Minnesota. Chicago: Geo. A. Ogle, 1900. Minnesota Reflections. https://reflections.mndigital.org/catalog/grh:54.

Strassburg, Herman A. *Call Book of Modern Quadrilles*. Detroit: American Music, 1889. Library of Congress. https://www.loc.gov/item/musdi.153/.

Stulen, Jo[h]n. "Dansemusikk for fiolin (og bass)." National Library of Norway, Mus.ms. 4689. https://urn.nb.no/URN:NBN:no-nb_digimanus_306932. This manuscript appears to date from approximately 1889 to 1906.

Svien, Orvin. "The Fiddle." Collection of Beth Hoven Rotto.

Toll, Robert C. *Blacking Up: The Minstrel Show in Nineteenth-Century America*. New York: Oxford University Press, 1974.

Tucker, Henry. *Clog Dancing Made Easy: The Elements and Practice of That Art Arranged, Simplified, and Corrected, with Examples*. New York: Robert M. De Witt, 1874. Library of Congress. https://www.loc.gov/item/05029186/.

Ulvestad, Martin. *Norge i Amerika med kart: Oplysninger om de norske Amerikanere*. Minneapolis: Norge i Amerika Publishing, 1901. National Library of Norway. https://urn.nb.no/URN:NBN:no-nb_digibok_2006112101031.

Ursin, [Niels Kristiansen]. "Danser." National Library of Norway, Mus.ms.a 2427. https://urn.nb.no/URN:NBN:no-nb_digimanus_175585.

Veflingstad, M. *Stange bygdebok*. Vol. 1, *Gårds- og slektshistorien*. [Stange, Norway]: Historielag, 1951.

"Veteran Fiddlers Recall Days of the Old Round Dances and Dance Calls." *Minneapolis Morning Tribune*, February 15, 1914. Minnesota Digital Newspaper Hub. https://www.mnhs.org/newspapers/lccn/sn83016772/1914-02-15/ed-1/seq-13.

Vollsnes, Arvid O., ed. *Norges musikkhistorie*. Vol. 3, *1870–1910: Romantikk og Gullalder*, edited by Finn Benestad, Nils Grinde, and Harald Herresthal. Oslo: Aschehoug, 1999.

Vollsnes, Arvid O. "Norway–Music and Musical Life." In *Norway: Society and Culture*, 2nd ed., edited by Eva Maagerø and Birte Simonsen, 279–305. Kristiansand: Portal Books, 2008.

[Wesson, Katharine?]. "Early Trails and Roads Leading to La Crosse." Hand-drawn map showing roads existing during the nineteenth century, ca. 1935. University of Wisconsin Digital Collections. https://digital.library.wisc.edu/1711 .dl/V4MBV5V4EQZCJ8K.

Ziener, Torgeir. "Anders Sørensen." In *Store norske leksikon*. Last updated February 13, 2009. https://nbl.snl.no/Anders_Sørensen.

Zikoff, F[riedrich]. *Life Is a Dream*. Arranged by W. F. Sudds. Boston: Oliver Ditson, 1879. Library of Congress. https://www.loc.gov/item/sm1879.13868/.

Zikoff, F[riedrich]. *Life Is a Dream*. Boston: White, Smith, ca.1876–1887. https://hdl.handle.net/2027/mdp.39015097846078.

Genealogical Records

Records Related to Thor Balstad

Baptismal record for Gustava Marie Balstad [daughter of Thor Balstad], Valders and G. Jerpen Lutheran Parish, Valders, Wisconsin, May 19, 1867. Digital image accessed from U.S. Evangelical Lutheran Church in America Church Records, 1781–1969 database on Ancestry.com.

Census record for Thor Larsen [Balstad], Nes Parish, Hedmark, Norway, 1865. Data accessed from Folketelling 1865 for 0411P Nes prestegjeld database in Digitalarkivet service of the National Archives of Norway. https://www.digitalarkivet.no/census/person/pf01038030001592.

Confirmation record for Clara Enanda Balstad [daughter of Thor Balstad], Valders and G. Jerpen Lutheran Parish, Valders, Wisconsin, May 4, 1879. Digital image accessed from U.S. Evangelical Lutheran Church in America Church Records, 1781–1969 database on Ancestry.com.

Records Related to Ole Hendricks

1885 Dakota Territorial Census, Walcott, Richland County, p. 26. June 13, 1885. North Dakota State University Archives, microfilm roll 7837, p. 122. Digital image accessed from North Dakota, Territorial and State Censuses, 1885, 1915, 1925 database on Ancestry.com, s.v. "Henrikson, Ole."

Baptismal record for Ole, son of Andreas Henriksen and Helge Olsdatter, Sauherad Parish, Telemark, Norway, March 9, 1851. Digital image of Klokkerbok nr. I 2, 1842–66, p. 46 accessed from Digitalarkivet service of National Archives of Norway. https://www.arkivverket.no/URN:NBN:no-a1450-kb20061211310035 .jpg. [Birth date February 19, 1851.]

Emigration record for Andreas Henriksen and family, Sauherad Parish, Telemark, Norway, 1854. Digital image of Ministerialbok nr. I 7, 1851–73, p. 254 accessed from Digitalarkivet service of National Archives of Norway. https://urn.digital arkivet.no/URN:NBN:no-a1450-kb20061127340243.jpg.

Records Related to Hans Samuelstad

1880 United States Census, Pigeon Township, Trempealeau County, Wisconsin, population schedule, p. 5, dwelling 44, family 45. June 4, 1880. National Archives microfilm roll 1448, p. 104A. Digital image accessed on Ancestry.com, s.v. "Semulstad, [*sic*] Hans O."

Burial record for Hans O. Samuelstad, Whitehall Lutheran Church, Whitehall, Wisconsin, November 30, 1892. Digital image accessed from U.S. Evangelical

Lutheran Church in America Church Records, 1781–1969 database on Ancestry. com. [Death date November 27, 1892.]

Homestead Certificate no. 4451 issued April 20, 1882 to Hans O. Samuelstad by General Land Office in La Crosse, Wisconsin. United States Bureau of Land Management, General Land Office Records, Federal Land Patents, State Volumes, Wisconsin. Digital image accessed from U.S. General Land Office Records, 1776–2015 database on Ancestry.com.

Records Related to Martinus Nilsen Spangberg

Burial record for Martinus Nilsen Spangberg, Stange Parish, Hedmark, Norway, February 14, 1898. Data accessed from Klokkerbok for Stange prestegjeld, Ottestad sokn 1894–1905 (0417P) database in Digitalarkivet service of the National Archives of Norway. https://www.digitalarkivet.no/view/267/pg0000 0001695954. [Indicates birth date as 1829, death date as February 6, 1898.]

Records Related to Andreas Tomta (Andrew Thorson)

1895 Minnesota State Census, Minneapolis—Ward 3, Hennepin County, p. 51. June 11, 1895. Minnesota Historical Society, Minnesota State Population Census Schedules, 1865–1905, microfilm roll V290_64. Data accessed from the Minnesota, Territorial and State Censuses, 1849–1905 database on Ancestry.com, s.v. "Thorson, Andrew."

Death record for Andrew Thorson, Minneapolis, Hennepin County, Minnesota, July 2, 1912. Data accessed from Minnesota Deaths and Burials, 1835–1990 database in FamilySearch. https://familysearch.org/ark:/61903/1:1:FD96-W86.

Records related to Anton Tømten

1900 United States Census, Coon, Vernon County, Wisconsin, population schedule, dwelling 46, family 46. June 5–6, 1900. National Archives microfilm. Digital image accessed on Ancestry.com, s.v. "Tomten, Anton."

Records related to D. O. Wold

Marriage record for Dyre Ols Vold (Friisvold), Stange Parish, Hedmark, Norway, May 2, 1860. Data accessed from Ministerialbok for Stange prestegjeld 1852–1862 (0417P) database in Digitalarkivet service of the National Archives of Norway. https://www.digitalarkivet.no/en/view/327/pv00000002354942.

Out-migration record for Even Olsen [brother of Dyre Olsen Wold], Stange Parish, Hedmark, Norway, April 15, 1854. Data accessed from Ministerialbok for Stange prestegjeld 1852–1862 (0417P) database in Digitalarkivet service of the National Archives of Norway. https://www.digitalarkivet.no/view/291/pu000 00000086668.

Music Recordings

Anders Grøthes Ensemble. *Danser i gammel stil av Anders Sørensen og Ole Rønning.* Aksent AKSCD022, 2019. https://open.spotify.com/album/1CrMrH8yMvgKR LaVhMRSTR.

Birger Lundbys Ensemble. *Hedemarksmusikk: Birger Lundbys ensemble spiller gamle danser.* Talent Produksjon TLS 3055, 1979, 33⅓ rpm. https://open.spotify.com/album/2Ru5uvSQDgKiXhXfFdo5kp.

Faukstad, Jon. *Norske drag: Folkemusikk på akkordeon.* Heilo HCD 7086, 1993. https://open.spotify.com/album/5727HyTXceKyQDZpFNTZxO.

Faukstad, Jon, and Per Sæmund Bjørkum. *Slåtter frå Torger Olstads notebok.* Bergen Digital Studio BD7018CD, 1995. https://open.spotify.com/album/2tOu G5OoMHLeopTtOY7umY.

Foot-Notes. *My Father Was a Fiddler.* Released 1998. Compact disc.

Jabbour, Alan, ed. *American Fiddle Tunes from the Archive of Folk Song.* Folk Music of the United States. Library of Congress Music Division, Recording Laboratory AFS L62, released 1971, 33⅓ rpm. Audio recordings available at https://www.loc.gov/item/2016655239/; booklet available at https://www.loc.gov/folk life/LP/AmFiddleTunesLiner_opt.pdf.

Korneliussen, Kåre, and Harry Borgen. *Trekkspillvirtuosene Kåre Korneliussen og Harry Borgen: Duettinnspillinger fra 1970-tallet.* Aksent AKSCD 0008, released 2016, compact disc. https://open.spotify.com/album/0fixMGpZtcsj13KloxPSw6.

Leary, James P. *Folksongs of Another America: Field Recordings from the Upper Midwest, 1937–1946.* Madison: University of Wisconsin Press and Dust-to-Digital, 2015. Audio recordings available at https://uwdc.library.wisc.edu/collections/localcenters/fsoaa/

The New Ole Hendricks Orchestra. *Play It Again, Ole!* NewOle001, 2019, compact disc and digital distribution. https://northernlightstrad.com/.

Norske Turdansar: Kontradansar frå Austlandet; By- og Storgårdsmusikk frå 1800-talet. Heilo HCD 7089, 1994, compact disc. Includes tracks performed by Bas og Bordun and Christiania Thour- og Runddansensemble. https://open.spot ify.com/album/4CRprlUQaFw7rMpUlkzlJ9.

Norwegian-American Music from Minnesota: Old-Time and Traditional Favorites. Produced by Philip Nusbaum. Minnesota Historical Society Press, released 1989, 33⅓ rpm.

Odde, Bjørn Kåre, and Ole Nilssen. *Hand.* Ta:lik TA206CD, 2019, compact disc.

Over Stok og Steen. *Over Stok og Steen.* Heilo HCD7141, 1998, compact disc. Notes by Thomas Nilssen.

Over Stok og Steen. *Til almuen.* 2L 2L15, 2003, compact disc. Notes by Ronny Kjøsen and Thomas Nilssen. http://www.2l.no/artists/2L15artist.htm.

Parker, Chet. *The Hammer Dulcimer Played by Chet Parker*. Folkways Records FA 2381, 1966, 33⅓ rpm.

Tunes from the Amerika Trunk: Traditional Norwegian-American Music from Wisconsin, volume 2. Produced by Philip Martin. Wisconsin Folklife Center—Folklore Village Farm Records FVF 202, released 1984, 33⅓ rpm.

NEWSPAPERS

Grant County Herald. Elbow Lake, Minnesota. 1890–1911. Accessed at the Minnesota Historical Society.

Richland County Gazette. Wahpeton, Dakota Territory. 1885–89. Accessed at the State Historical Society of North Dakota.

Wahpeton Times. Wahpeton, Dakota Territory. 1884–89. Library of Congress, Chronicling America. https://chroniclingamerica.loc.gov/lccn/sn84024779/issues/.

Index

The letter *t* following page numbers indicate a tune transcription. Page numbers in italics indicate an illustration.

Languages and Folklore of the Upper Midwest

JOSEPH SALMONS AND JAMES P. LEARY, *Series Editors*

Songs of the Finnish Migration: A Bilingual Anthology
Edited by THOMAS A. DUBOIS and B. MARCUS CEDERSTRÖM

*Folksongs of Another America: Field Recordings from the
Upper Midwest, 1937–1946*
JAMES P. LEARY

The Tamburitza Tradition: From the Balkans to the American Midwest
RICHARD MARCH

Wisconsin Talk: Linguistic Diversity in the Badger State
Edited by THOMAS PURNELL, ERIC RAIMY, and JOSEPH SALMONS

Yooper Talk: Dialect as Identity in Michigan's Upper Peninsula
KATHRYN A. REMLINGER

Pinery Boys: Songs and Songcatching in the Lumberjack Era
Edited by FRANZ RICKABY with GRETCHEN DYKSTRA
and JAMES P. LEARY

*Ole Hendricks and His Tunebook: Folk Music and
Community on the Frontier*
AMY M. SHAW